LEAVING A GODLY

LEGACY

CHARLES
STANLEY

OLIVER
NELSON
™

THOMAS NELSON PUBLISHERS
Nashville

Published in Nashville, Tennessee, by Thomas Nelson, Inc.

Unless otherwise noted, Scripture quotations are from THE NEW KING JAMES VERSION. Copyright © 1979, 1980, 1982, Thomas Nelson, Inc., Publishers.

Scripture quotations noted KJV are from the KING JAMES VERSION.

Scripture quotations noted NIV are from the Holy Bible: NEW INTERNA-TIONAL VERSION®. Copyright© 1973, 1978, 1984 by International Bible Society. Used by permission of Zondervan Publishing House. All rights reserved.

ISBN 0-7852-7289-5

Printed in the United States of America
03 04 05 06 07 — 05 04 03 02 01

CONTENTS

INTRODUCTION

THE INHERITANCE THAT REALLY MATTERS

W hen most of us think about leaving or receiving an "inheritance," we automatically think in terms of money and property, including personal items of sentimental value. The Bible presents a much more important legacy that we as Christian parents, grandparents, and mature Christian adults are to leave to our children. It is the legacy that lies in the emotional and spiritual realms—a legacy of lifelong benefit and eternal value.

Much of what we know in the Scriptures about leaving a godly legacy can be found in the writings of Paul the apostle. It is Paul who spelled out in clear terms how Christians are to express their belief in Christ Jesus and especially how Christians are to treat one another. Paul uses two phrases that deserve our attention at the outset of our discussion about legacy.

Live a life worthy of our calling. The word *worthy* may also be translated as "weighty." Paul called upon Christians to leave a weighty imprint wherever they walked. Imagine for a moment that a person is walking through a slab of wet concrete. The heavier the person, the deeper and more distinct the footprints that are going to be created. As believers in Christ Jesus, we are not to wander aimlessly through life or to have futility in our thinking. We are to walk with purpose, intending to leave a deep imprint on the lives of all we touch—especially so, on our children.

This imprint is not only to be "weighty" but it is to be lasting. We are to leave a permanent imprint upon our children.

Finally, this weighty imprint we leave is to be one that is directly related to our calling. What is our calling? This word does not refer to a full-time ministry vocation or to a specific call of God to undertake a particular project or task. Our calling is to be Christlike. As Paul wrote to the Philippians, "I press toward the goal for the prize of the upward call of God in Christ Jesus" (Phil. 3:14). Our calling is to a higher morality, a higher ethical standard, a higher spiritual plane, a higher way of living—one that culminates in our walking in righteousness every day of our lives and then walking into our perfection in heaven.

We are to leave a weighty, permanent imprint of God's love, goodness, and forgiveness wherever we walk, for as long as we walk on this earth.

Imitators of Christ. Paul states in Ephesians 5:1, "Be imitators of God . . . as dearly loved children" (NIV) The legacy that we leave to our children is to be one of Christlikeness. To be an imitator of Christ is to "mimic" Christ—not in a mocking way, but in a "mirroring" way. We are to copy Him. To be a follower of Christ Jesus means that we are to develop the same character Christ Jesus displayed, relate to other people as Christ Jesus related to them, and to obey God the Father as Christ Jesus obeyed Him. We are to love sacrificially and to pour out our lives in service to those whom God causes to cross our path.

In every aspect of our attitude, conversation, and behavior, we are to imitate Christ to our children.

What is the nature of the emotional and spiritual legacy we

are to leave behind? It is a weighty, permanent imprint of Christ Jesus upon their lives.

How Children Learn

In writing to the Ephesians regarding imitators of God, Paul stated a very important concept: we are to be "as dear children." Paul knew that children learn first by copying the behavior of their parents. We have all seen a little child who walks just like his daddy walks or tosses her head just like her mother. Children learn most of what they learn by imitating others. They learn to talk, walk, handle objects, and behave toward other people as they see their parents talking, walking, handling objects, and behaving toward others.

A baby has the potential to learn any language—but the language your child learns is the language you speak, including your inflections, accent, and vocabulary.

A baby has the potential to walk—but when and how that baby walks is directly related to the way the parents demonstrate to that child how to walk.

A newborn baby has the potential to learn to use chopsticks or a fork—whichever you use, your child will learn to use. And the same is true for everything from tying shoelaces to using a toothbrush.

The way you treat other people is going to be the way your child treats them. The attitudes you have are going to be the first attitudes your child has. The nature of your conversation is going to become the nature of your child's conversation.

What an awesome responsibility a parent has to be an "imitator of Christ"—because as the parent imitates Christ, the child is going to imitate the parent. It is in this way that children "learn Christ." They learn how to be a Christian and what it means to accept Christ, follow Christ, and develop a personal relationship with Christ first and foremost from their parents.

Never Forgotten

A material or financial legacy can be squandered, misused, or spent. An emotional and spiritual legacy may be ignored or rebelled against by a child, but it can never be forgotten. How you live is a legacy that will always be with your child, for better or worse.

What you do will always be more powerful than what you say. For a legacy to have maximum impact, beliefs must line up with words, which in turn must line up with deeds. There must be a consistency of Christlikeness throughout a parent's life if the spiritual legacy of a parent is going to be of greatest value.

The question naturally arises: "What are the things that are most important for me to leave my children as an emotional and spiritual legacy?" This question is at the heart of this Bible study. While there may be other things worthy of your giving to your child, in this study we will take a look at what I believe to be the foundation stones of a godly legacy. A child who receives the emotional and spiritual legacy identified in this book is going to be a child who has all that is necessary for living a godly, moral, Christ-centered, wise, strong, loving, and eternal life.

Spiritual Children, Too

You may not be a parent or grandparent. You may be an aunt or uncle, a godmother or godfather, or perhaps you are a teacher, child-care provider, or someone who works regularly with children. You may simply be a Christian adult in the body of Christ. This book is for you, too!

Each of us as mature Christians is called to leave a godly legacy to all who see our lives, and that includes the lives of children we may not even know. It also includes the lives of those who are our "spiritual children"—the children of all ages whom we lead to Christ and help nurture and raise up to maturity in Christ. The legacy you leave to your spiritual children is no less important than the legacy left by parents to their natural-born or adopted children.

Ask God today to help you identify specific children in your life to whom you desire to leave a godly legacy. Keep these children in mind as you do this study. They will help make it even more personal and meaningful to you.

And now as you prepare to begin this study, I invite you to consider these questions:

- When you hear the word *legacy*, what comes to your mind?

- What type of emotional legacy do you desire to leave the children whom God has given to you to love and nurture (including spiritual children)?

- What type of spiritual legacy do you desire to leave the children in your life?

ONE

PLACING PRIORITY ON A SPIRITUAL LEGACY

The Bible is the most practical, down-to-earth book on parenting that has ever been written. It covers every area of raising godly children, including what it means to leave a godly legacy.

People, however, seem to have two questions when it comes to what the Bible has to say about parenting: they wonder if what the Bible has to say is for *this* generation, and they wonder about their own capacity to be a good parent.

Let me assure you that the Bible is for today. No situation or circumstance that your family encounters is different *in nature* from the situations and circumstances encountered by families in biblical times. Technology and the amount of available information on any given topic may have changed dramatically, but the human heart has not changed. Parents and children still face the same challenges in their emotional and spiritual lives that parents and children faced thousands of years ago.

Let me also reassure you that you *can* be a godly parent and leave a good spiritual and emotional legacy to your children, regardless of what may have happened to you as a child. You do not need to repeat the bad habits of your own parents or be a victim of the "generational curses" that seem to plague your family as a whole. God desires to free you from the bad teaching that you may have received and to heal you of hurts you may have experienced as a child. You do not need to imitate your own parents—rather, you can imitate your heavenly Father in your child-rearing. God desires for you to be able to love your children in purity and freedom and to train them to walk in righteousness before Him. No teaching of the Bible is ever considered to be off-limits or inapplicable to any Christian. As believers in Christ Jesus, we each have a capacity to conform our lives to the Bible's truth, and we each have access to the Holy Spirit to help us daily to live a godly life.

As you study God's principles for a godly legacy, I encourage you to go again and again to your Bible and to underline phrases, highlight words or verses, and make notes in the margins of your Bible to record the specific ways God speaks to you as a parent. I believe in a well-marked Bible. My Bible is filled with dates, notes, and insights. Since the application of God's Word is always very personal and direct, I especially encourage you to take note of the specific ways in which God admonishes, encourages, or directs *you*.

For Personal or Group Study

This Bible study book can be used by you alone or by several people in a small-group setting. If you are using this book for a personal Bible study, you will find places from time to time in which to note your insights or to respond to questions. If you are using the book for a small-group study, you also may use these questions and insight portions for group discussion.

At various times, you will be asked to relate to the material in these ways:

- What new insights have you gained?
- Have you ever had a similar experience?

- How do you feel about the material presented?
- In what way do you feel challenged to respond or to act?

Insights

An insight is more than a fact or idea. It is seeing something as if it is new to you. Most of us have had the experience of reading a passage of the Bible—perhaps even a passage that we have read dozens of times—and saying, "I never saw that before!" It may be a particular word or phrase that catches your eye. It may be that you suddenly see how that passage is linked to another passage in God's Word. It may be that you suddenly understand more fully what it is that God is desiring to teach you or show you.

Insights are usually highly individualized. They generally relate to our personal lives. We tend to see things in a new light because of circumstances or situations that we have recently encountered or are currently experiencing. At times, insights help us solve problems, answer questions, or resolve difficulties in a relationship. At times, they give specific direction about what to do or how to think. At times, they bolster faith.

Ask the Lord to speak to you personally every time you open His Word. I believe He will be faithful in answering your prayer.

As you experience insights, make notes about them. You may want to write these notes in your Bible or in a separate journal. The more you record insights, the more you are likely to have insights. In other words, the more you look and listen for God to speak to you, the more He does. In fact, if you haven't gained new spiritual insights after reading several passages from God's Word, you probably haven't been engaged in the process of study or haven't focused your attention on what you are reading.

From time to time in this book, you will be asked to note what a passage of the Bible is saying to you. These are times for recording your personal response or insight, not for summarizing a group response or what someone else in your Bible study group said. Make sure the insight or response is your own.

One of the most amazing things about spiritual insights is that the more we experience them, the more enthusiastic we tend to become about studying the Bible—and, the more we study God's Word with a desire to apply it to our lives, the deeper our relationship grows with the Lord.

Experience

Each of us comes to God's Word from a unique background. Nobody else has our particular set of past experiences or relationships. Each of us has a unique perspective on what we read in God's Word. We filter what we read about good parenting and leaving a godly legacy through our own childhood experiences.

Differing levels and types of experience can create problems in group Bible studies, although this is not necessarily so. For example, a person who had a very troubled childhood and who only recently started attending church is going to have a different perspective from a person who grew up in a Christian home and who has attended church and read the Bible all of his life.

What we need to recognize in a group setting is that we all have certain *common* life experiences. For example, we each can point to times in which we have felt troubled, lonely, inadequate, rejected, joyful, relieved, or appreciated. Focus on common experiences in your Bible study group. These are experiences that truly touch the deepest chords in the human heart.

We also must recognize that we each have experiences about which we can say, "Here's how that truth in the Bible displayed itself in my life," or "Here's what happened to me to convince me that God's Word is true."

Our experiences, of course, do not make the Bible true. The Bible is truth. The importance of noting and sharing our experiences is that we discover the many ways in which God's truth can be applied to human lives and circumstances. In sharing our life experiences, we see how God speaks personally and directly to each person. We discover a wider spectrum of needs, questions, and situations that are addressed by the Bible. We see that God's Word is not only universal, but also very specific. We nearly always come to the conclusion that our greatest potential for harmony and unity lies in each person's having a relationship with Christ Jesus and a desire to live according to God's principles. The Lord and His Word tie us together with bonds that cannot be broken.

Sharing experiences is significant for spiritual growth. If you are doing this study on your own, find someone with whom you can share your faith experience. Be open to hearing about that person's faith experiences in return.

Emotional Response

Just as we each have a personal catalog of life experiences, so each of us has a set of emotional responses. Face your emotions honestly. Be willing to share your emotional responses to God's Word, and allow others to share their responses without judgment or comment. One person may be overjoyed or feel encouraged after reading a particular passage of the Bible. Another person may respond to that same passage with perplexity or an unsettled feeling in the pit of their stomach.

Few areas are as emotion-laden as memories of our childhood and our concerns about the job we are doing as parents. Most people can recall with great clarity and impact the way they *felt* at certain times in their childhoods—for example,

- when Mom or Dad didn't show up right on time;
- when you forgot your lunch money and didn't know what to do;
- when you had to admit to your parents that you had told a lie.

We not only remember what happened, but how we felt. These emotions are often very strong and in some cases, they continue to have a powerful impact on the way we think and behave toward our own children.

What we need to recognize about our emotions is that we not only filter the Scriptures through our past experiences but also through our emotions. We read the Bible with an emotional response.

Our emotional responses do not give validity to the Scriptures, nor should we trust emotions as a measuring device for faith. Your faith must be based on what God says, not on how you feel. Recognizing how you feel about the truth of God's Word has this great benefit to you: it can lead you into a deeper study of the Bible to discover *why* you feel as you do and what *God* desires to do in your life. When we acknowledge our emotional response to a particular passage of God's Word, we often put ourselves into a greater position to be healed in our emotions or to be challenged to grow and mature in our spiritual walk.

In most small-group settings, I have found it much more beneficial for people to express their emotions than their opinions. Opinions tend to divide; the sharing of emotional responses tends to unite. The Holy Spirit often speaks to us in the unspoken language of promptings, intuition, emotions, and deep desires and longings. When we share feelings with one another, we not only open ourselves to deeper insights into God's Word but also grow closer together as members of the body of Christ. A sense of community develops, and we understand more clearly what it means to be "one in the Spirit." It is through the sharing of joys and sorrows, assurances and doubts, hopes and fears, that we mature as individuals and as churches.

Challenges

As we read God's Word, we nearly always feel conviction at some point—as if God is speaking directly to us. We may feel challenged to change something we are presently doing, to take a new step, or to make a new start. At times, we may feel challenged to continue steadfastly in the direction we are going or to stand firm in our faith. These moments of conviction can be very strong. They may occur once or repeatedly, but they are impossible to ignore or escape.

I am saying this to alert you to the fact that as you study God's Word about leaving a godly legacy, you are likely to feel that you have "fallen short" of God's ideal. Your first impulse may be to close your Bible, close this book, and walk away with feelings of defeat. Don't give in to that impulse! Stay with your study and get the whole of God's message. Consider this study a part of God's "development" process in making you into the parent He desires for you to be.

I believe we gain a great deal by writing down the ways in which we believe God is stretching us, molding us, calling us, or causing us to believe for more. When we identify clearly and succinctly what God wants us to do and be, we are in a much better position to take action that is responsible, measured, and deliberate. We are to *respond* to God's Word, not merely react to it. God expects us to become *doers* of His Word, not hearers only (see James 1:22).

Ultimately, God desires to get His Word into us and us into His Word so we can take His Word into the world, live it out, and be witnesses of His Word in all we say and do. We are to be God's living letter to an unsaved world about how to live a godly life and leave a godly legacy to our children.

Confidentiality

Especially when it comes to dealing with family issues, you must make certain that every person in your small group is committed to the confidentiality of the group. What you share in the group setting should remain within the group. Be aware that you must guard against a tendency to brag about ways in which God is blessing members of your family, or to air the particular faults and shortcomings of a spouse or child. This is not a place to "expose" the sins or secrets of other family members. Be sensitive to how you would feel if your family members were telling your sins or secrets! Make certain that what you share in the group is *your* insight, *your* experience, *your* emotional response, or *your* challenge from God. Talk about yourself only, not other family members.

Keep the Bible Central

Again, I caution you to keep the Bible at the center of your study. Otherwise, your group may become a therapy or support group of some type. It is as we gather around God's Word—to feed upon it, learn from it, and grow into it—that we truly grow spiritually and put ourselves into a position to leave a godly legacy.

If you are doing a personal Bible study, you also must be diligent in staying focused on God's Word. Self-analysis and introspection are not the goals of this study. Growing into the fullness of the stature of Christ Jesus is the goal!

Prayer

I encourage you to begin and end your Bible study sessions in prayer. Ask God to give you spiritual eyes to see what He wants you to see and spiritual ears to hear what He wants you to hear. Ask Him to give you new insights, to recall to your memory the experiences that will help you in your spiritual growth, and to help you identify your emotions clearly. Be bold in asking Him to reveal to you from His Word what He desires for you to take as the next step toward leaving a godly legacy to your children.

As you conclude a time of study, ask the Lord to seal to your heart and mind what you have learned so you will never forget it. Ask Him to transform you more into the likeness of Christ Jesus.

The Depth of God's Word

Avoid the temptation of concluding at the end of your ten-week study that you have all the information you need to leave a godly legacy. In all likelihood, you have only begun this journey. Continue to read and study God's Word and to grow in your understanding of God's truth.

- *What new insights about parenting do you anticipate God may have for you personally and individually?*

  _____

  _____

- *In what areas do you struggle the most as a parent?*

  _____

  _____

- *Identify some of your fears as a parent—and also some of your hopes and joys.*

  _____

  _____

- *In what ways do you already feel the Lord challenging you in your spirit about the godly legacy He desires for you to leave to your children?*

  _____

  _____

TWO

A STRONG SENSE OF BELONGING

One of the greatest gifts you can ever give to your child is a strong sense of belonging—not only to your family but to the greater family of the Body of Christ.

Every parent knows that he or she needs to provide the "basics" for children—adequate food, shelter, clothing, safety. Equally important, however, is the need to provide the "basics" for the emotional well-being of a child. Emotional well-being begins with a sense of belonging.

A sense of belonging is the conclusion that a child draws that he is *wanted*. It includes feelings of being cared for, of being appreciated for his uniqueness, of being "enjoyed" for his personality.

A child who does not have a sense of belonging grows up feeling rejected and alienated from other people. Often, the tendency of a child who feels rejected is for that child to seek out those who do "want" him, even to the joining of a gang or cult. At times, a child who feels rejected spends years, even a lifetime, trying to prove that he is desirable.

• *Have you personally ever felt rejected? Have you had experiences in which you felt you didn't belong?*

- *As a child, did you feel fully that you belonged in your family? Did you have a sense of belonging fully to a church body?*

Of one thing we can be absolutely certain in the Scriptures is that God *wants* us. He created us, He desires us, He longs to be in close relationship with us. He seeks us out. He invites us to spend time with Him. God's purpose in saving us is so that we will live forever with Him in heaven.

Those who leave a godly legacy are those who never exclude other believers—regardless of their denomination—but who are quick to express their appreciation for the presence of other believers in their lives. The apostle Paul wrote to the Romans, "I long to see you, that I may impart to you some spiritual gift, so that you may be established—that is, that I may be encouraged together with you by the mutual faith both of you and me" (Rom. 1:11–12). He said to the Philippians, "For God is my witness, how greatly I long for you all with the affection of Jesus Christ" (Phil. 1:8). Later in his letter, Paul called the Philippians his "beloved and longed-for brethren" (Phil. 4:1). How good the believers in Rome and Philippi must have felt when they read these words from Paul!

- *How does it feel to hear someone say, "I can hardly wait to be with you"?*

What the Word Says

When You said, "Seek My face,"

What the Word Says to Me

My heart said to You, "Your
face, LORD, I will seek."
(Ps. 27:8)

[Jesus said of Himself], "The
Son of Man has come to seek
and to save that which was
lost." (Luke 19:10)

[Jesus said], "In My Father's
house are many mansions; if it
were not so, I would have told
you. I go to prepare a place for
you. And if I go and prepare a
place for you, I will come again
and receive you to Myself; that
where I am, there you may be
also." (John 14:2–3)

The LORD has appeared of old
to me, saying:
"Yes, I have loved you with an
everlasting love;
Therefore with lovingkindness
I have drawn you." (Jer. 31:3)

Creating a Sense of Belonging in Your Child

There are two main ways to build a sense of belonging in your child: spend time with your child, and ask your child for his ideas and opinions.

1. Give Your Child Time

Children *need* to spend time with their parents. They need to know that Mom and Dad are always available or accessible to them, even if it is by phone. From time to time, every child needs to spend time exclusively with his or her Mom and Dad. Children not only need "quality" time, they need vast quantities of time.

Never exclude your child from your presence without giving your child a specific *reason* you need to be alone or with another person, and a specific *time* when you will again be available to your child. Recognize that young children have short attention spans. Take the few seconds required to give your child the hug he needs, to answer the question he has, or to show appreciation to your child when he comes seeking your approval.

Jesus is our role model when it comes to taking time to be with children. In Jesus' day, little children were not highly regarded by most adults—many thought them unworthy of being included in religious gatherings until they were "of age." Jesus did not take that approach! We read in Matthew 19:13–14,

> Then little children were brought to Him that He might put His hands on them and pray, but the disciples rebuked them. But Jesus said, "Let the little children come to Me, and do not forbid them; for of such is the kingdom of heaven."

God's plan for the teaching of children was that children would be with their parents throughout a day, learning from their parents' example and from frequent, spur-of-the-moment conversations as various situations and problems arose. We read this in Deuteronomy:

> These words which I command you today shall be in your heart; you shall teach them diligently to your children, and shall talk of them when you sit in your house, when you walk by the way, when you lie down, and when you rise up. (Deut. 6:6–7)

God expected children to learn about His commandments and His great love through *being with their parents*—by hearing their parents speak of obedience to a loving God, and by watching their parents as they serve God.

When we spend time with our children, we convey to them the greater truth that God, their heavenly Father, always has time for them. He is always available to them, always desires to be with them, and always longs to be in an intimate, loving relationship with them.

- *What new insights do you have into these passages from Matthew and Deuteronomy?*

_____

_____

What the Word Says

What the Word Says to Me

As God has said:
"I will dwell in them
And walk among them.
I will be their God,
And they shall be My people."
(2 Cor. 6:16)

And Jesus, perceiving the thought of their heart, took a little child, and set him by Him, and said to them, "Whoever receives this little child in My name receives Me; and whoever receives Me receives Him who sent Me." (Luke 9:47–48)

- *In what ways are you feeling challenged in your spirit?*

_____

_____

2. Value your child's ideas and opinions.

A child feels included if his ideas and opinions are valued and sought out. On the other hand, if parents make all of the decisions, voice all of the opinions, and come up with all of the ideas in a family, a child begins to regard his presence in the family as being unwanted or unnecessary.

It is also vital that you give validity and importance to your child's questions. When you take time to answer your child's questions, you send the message to your child, "I want you to know what I know. I want to share a mutual life with you."

The Lord is never too tired or too busy to hear from us—to hear our petitions, our praises, our questions, our hopes, our desires.

What the Word Says	What the Word Says to Me
"Come now, and let us reason together," Says the LORD. (Isa. 1:18)	
Behold, the LORD's hand is not shortened, That it cannot save; Nor His ear heavy, That it cannot hear. (Isa. 59:1)	
Now as He sat on the Mount of Olives, the disciples came to Him privately, saying, "Tell us, when will these things be? And what will be the sign of Your coming, and of the end of the age?" And Jesus answered and said to them . . . (Matt. 24:3–4)	
And it came to pass, as He	

was praying in a certain place,
when He ceased, that one of
His disciples said to Him,
"Lord, teach us to pray, as
John also taught his disciples."
So He said to them . . . (Luke
11:1–2)

[Jesus said,] "The one who
comes to Me I will by no
means cast out." (John 6:37)

• *In what ways are you feeling challenged in your spirit?*

_____

_____

The Great Value God Places on "Belonging"

Throughout the New Testament, we find great value being placed on "belonging"—both to God and to the family of God, which is the Church. The apostle John stated in his Gospel that the very reason Jesus came to this earth was to show us what the Father is like and to show us that the Father desires to be in relationship with us: "The Word became flesh and dwelt among us, and we beheld His glory" (John 1:14). God desires that we belong to Him, to know Him, to be reconciled to Him.

Jesus was in close fellowship with His disciples. He broke bread with them, He walked with them, He invited them to participate fully in His ministry. His final prayer for them was that they—and us—might become *one* with Him.

What the Word Says

[Jesus prayed for His disciples,]
"And the glory which You gave

What the Word Says to Me

_____

_____

Me I have given them, that they may be one just as We are one: I in them, and You in Me; that they may be made perfect in one, and that the world may know that You have sent Me, and have loved them as You have loved Me." (John 17:22–23)

[Paul wrote,] I, therefore, the prisoner of the Lord, beseech you to have a walk worthy of the calling with which you were called, with all lowliness and gentleness, with longsuffering, bearing with one another in love, endeavoring to keep the unity of the Spirit in the bond of peace. There is one body and one Spirit, just as you were called in one hope of your calling; one Lord, one faith, one baptism; one God and Father of all, who is above all, and through all, and in you all. (Eph. 4:1–6)

God's plan was for the church to be a community that lived in unity of Spirit. Every believer was expected to be linked to every other believer in "one body" and "one faith." Jesus taught this clearly:

"Again I say to you that if two of you agree on earth concerning anything that they ask, it will be done for them by My Father in heaven. For where two or three are gathered together in My name, I am there in the midst of them." (Matt. 18:19–20)

Within the church, every believer should be made to feel at "home" and part of the family—no believer should be excluded.

What the Word Says	What the Word Says to Me
That which we have seen and heard we declare to you, that you also may have fellowship with us; and truly our fellowship is with the Father and with His Son Jesus Christ. (1 John 1:3)	----------------------------------- ----------------------------------- ----------------------------------- ----------------------------------- ----------------------------------- ----------------------------------- -----------------------------------
My brethren, do not hold the faith of our Lord Jesus Christ, the Lord of glory, with partiality. For if there should come into your assembly a man with gold rings, in fine apparel, and there should also come in a poor man in filthy clothes, and you pay attention to the one wearing the fine clothes and say to him, "You sit here in a good place," and say to the poor man, "You stand there," or, "Sit here at my footstool," have you not shown partiality among yourselves, and become judges with evil thoughts? Listen, my beloved brethren: Has God not	----------------------------------- ----------------------------------- ----------------------------------- ----------------------------------- ----------------------------------- ----------------------------------- ----------------------------------- ----------------------------------- ----------------------------------- ----------------------------------- ----------------------------------- ----------------------------------- ----------------------------------- ----------------------------------- ----------------------------------- ----------------------------------- -----------------------------------

chosen the poor of this world to be rich in faith and heirs of the kingdom which He promised to those who love Him? . . . If you show partiality, you commit sin. (James 2:1–5, 9)

For you are all sons of God through faith in Christ Jesus. For as many of you as were baptized into Christ have put on Christ. There is neither Jew nor Greek, there is neither slave nor free, there is neither male nor female; for you are all one in Christ Jesus. (Gal. 3:26–28)

When we give to our children a strong sense that they belong to us as parents, and belong to our families as vital, worthy members, we give to our children a great foundation on which they can begin to learn all that it means to *belong* to God. We give them the desire to belong to God. We give them the firm footing they need to see themselves as *belonging* fully in the Body of Christ, and of extending full membership and a sense of belonging to all other believers in the Church.

"To belong" is a great and godly legacy we can and must give to our children!

- *What new insights do you have into the godly legacy the Lord desires you to give your children?*

- *In what ways are you feeling challenged in your spirit?*

THREE

A STRONG SENSE OF VALUE

Everybody needs to feel loved—to feel that he or she has value in another person's eyes. To be loved is to gain self-worth.

Unconditional love creates self-esteem in a child; conditional love based on "ifs," "whens," and "buts" creates self-doubt. The earlier a person experiences unconditional love in his or her life, the more solid the foundation for that person's emotional development and well-being.

One of the greatest messages you can ever convey to your child is this: "I love you solely because you are *you*. I thank God that He created you and put you into my life."

> • *Have you experienced unconditional love in your life? From whom? What was the effect or result?*

_____

_____

A message of unconditional love is also interpreted by a child that the child is "lovable"—not only to other people, but to God. The child who experiences unconditional love is far less likely to perceive God as a harsh, punitive judge and far more likely to perceive God as a loving, giving, merciful Heavenly Father.

• *How do you feel when you think about God? Is your immediate response to God one of openness and love, or do you feel fear, anxiety, or reluctance to approach God?*

_____

_____

One of the greatest gifts you can ever give to a child is a perception of God as a loving, forgiving Father. Such a perception makes it far more likely that your child is going to desire to communicate with God, grow in their relationship with God, and turn to God in any time of crisis or need.

What the Word Says	What the Word Says to Me
We have known and believed the love that God has for us. God is love, and he who abides in love abides in God, and God in him. (1 John 4:16)	_____ _____ _____ _____ _____
[Jesus said,] "For God *so loved the world* that He gave His only begotten Son, that whoever believes in Him should not perish but have everlasting life." (John 3:16, emphasis mine)	_____ _____ _____ _____ _____ _____

• *Have you accepted God's love for you?*

_____

_____

Freedom to love. The child who experiences unconditional love is much freer in expressing love to other people. In fact, a person who has not experienced unconditional love has a great deal of difficulty loving others. He or she has no basis for knowing how to love and is far more likely to be manipulative and controlling when it comes to matters of the heart. Relationships crumble and are destroyed when love is given conditionally with a constant undercurrent of "I'll love you if you . . .", or "I love you when you . . .", or "I can't love you unless you . . ."

Unless a person receives God's unconditional love, that person cannot love as God loves. God's loving poured into us and *through us* enables us to accept and to love fully.

- *Have you known people who had difficulty loving others unconditionally? Have you, yourself, had this difficulty?*

_____

_____

What the Word Says	What the Word Says to Me
If we love one another, God abides in us, and His love has been perfected in us. (1 John 4:12)	
We love Him because He first loved us. (1 John 4:19)	
[Jesus said,] "This is My commandment, that you love one another as I have loved you." (John 15:12)	

Three Results of Unconditional Love

Apart from having an ability and freedom to love others, unconditional love produces three things in your child that are of great benefit throughout your child's life: a genuine spontaneity in giving to others, to the point of self-sacrifice; an increased ability to trust God; and a greater desire to keep God's commandments.

1. Sacrificial giving.

Genuine love is always sacrificial love. Jesus is certainly our role model in this. He loved to the point of giving His life so that those who believe in Him might not receive sin's consequence of death, but rather, receive eternal life.

Parents, too, are called to give sacrificially to their children—to put the child's needs above their own needs and to give sacrificially of their time and energy. This does not mean that a parent should strive to provide all of a child's *wants*. True love also means doing what is *best* for a child in all situations, and it is never *best* to give a child everything the child desires. A child needs to earn some things he wants; a child needs to wait for some things he desires. A child should never have to wait or earn, however, an expression of a parent's love: a smile, an encouraging word, a hug, or the spoken words, "I love you."

Sacrificial giving on the part of a parent includes making the effort to attend your child's games or performances, even if you are exhausted . . . going to church with your child *every Sunday*, even if you'd rather sleep in or play golf . . . taking time to read to, play with, and pray with your child, even if you still feel that there is work you should get done that day . . . taking time to listen to your child, answer questions, and comfort your child, even if it means asking another adult to wait for you.

Paul wrote to the Ephesians that our sacrificial loving—which is loving as Christ loved—produces a "sweet-smelling aroma" before God. In other words, sacrificial love is *pleasing* to God. It is a way of honoring Him and of responding in a right way to His sacrificial love for us.

The child who experiences sacrificial love learns by your example what it means to be a giving, unselfish person. Such a person can really be used by God in all types of ministry!

- *Have you ever been the recipient of sacrificial giving? How did you feel? What was your response to that kind of love?*

_____

_____

What the Word Says	What the Word Says to Me
Walk in love, as Christ also has loved us and given Himself for us, an offering and a sacrifice to God for a sweet-smelling aroma. (Eph. 5:2)	....
[Jesus said,] "Greater love has no one than this, than to lay down one's life for his friends." (John 15:13)	....

2. Trust in God.

It is much easier to trust someone when you know they love you unconditionally. This includes our ability to trust God: how much easier it is to trust an unconditionally loving heavenly Father to meet our needs and help us in every situation of life, than to trust a God whom we perceive to be unmerciful, harsh, and critical!

A person who cannot trust others, and who does not trust God, is miserable and feels they must "make" things happen, not only in their own lives but in the lives of others. Such a person often becomes manipulative and suspicious of the motives of others. At the same time, since no person ultimately can control everything, the person is likely to experience increasing disappointment, anxiety, frustration, and even discouragement and depression.

The person who is able to receive God's unconditional love believes, *God is on my side. He loves me and desires what is good for me. He is going to act in a way that is eternally beneficial to me.*

I can trust Him with this situation, this relationship, this circumstance . . . and all of my life.

The child who learns to trust is willing to take risks in sharing his or her personal testimony about God's love. Such a child is not afraid of criticism and rejection because he *knows* that the most important thing in life is God's love and forgiveness, and that God will always be present in his life—now and forever. Above all, a child who knows she is loved unconditionally and eternally by God is freed from the deep inner fear that plagues so many people in our stress-filled world. To be loved by God and to trust God are vital for a person to feel secure.

- *What has been your personal experience in trusting God?*

_____

_____

What the Word Says	What the Word Says to Me
And He said to them, "Which of you shall have a friend, and go to him at midnight and say to him, 'Friend, lend me three loaves; for a friend of mine has come to me on his journey, and I have nothing to set before him'; and he will answer from within and say, 'Do not trouble me; the door is now shut, and my children are with me in bed; I cannot rise and give to you'? . . . If a son asks for bread from any father among you, will he give him a stone? Or if he asks for a fish,	

will he give him a serpent instead of a fish? Or if he asks for an egg, will he offer him a scorpion? If you then, being evil, know how to give good gifts to your children, how much more will your heavenly Father give the Holy Spirit to those who ask Him!" (Luke 11:5–7, 11–13)

For God has not given us a spirit of fear, but of power and of love and of a sound mind. (2 Tim. 1:7)

There is no fear in love; but perfect love casts out fear, because fear involves torment. But he who fears has not been made perfect in love. (1 John 4:18)

Delight yourself also in the LORD,
And He shall give you the desires of your heart.
(Ps. 37:4)

3. Keeping God's commandments.

A loving parent always sets boundaries for a child—not to punish or to break the spirit of the child, but rather, to *keep* the child from those things that the parent knows will bring harm to the child. In the same way, our loving heavenly Father has given us His commandments. They are for our eternal *good*.

If a child grows up believing that a parent's love is based upon conditions—including the condition of "obedience"—

that child is going to resent a parent's rules and is very likely going to rebel against them. However, if a child grows up believing that a parent's love is unconditional and that any rules the parents have made are a by-product of the parents' great love for the child, that child is much more likely to obey.

Part of trusting God is trusting that God's commandments and laws are for our benefit. When we know that God's rules are for our *good*, we are much more likely to keep them!

The result of obedience to God, of course, is that we are in a position to receive all that the Lord may desire to give to us. The obedient person is a person God can trust with His greatest blessings.

- *Have you had experience with rebellion in your past? What were the consequences?*

_____

_____

What the Word Says

See, I have set before you today life and good, death and evil, in that I command you today to love the LORD your God, to walk in His ways, and to keep His commandments, His statutes, and His judgments, that you may live and multiply; and the LORD your God will bless you in the land which you go to possess . . . Therefore choose life, that both you and your descendants may live; that you may love the LORD your God, that you may

What the Word Says to Me

_____

_____

_____

_____

_____

_____

_____

_____

_____

_____

_____

_____

_____

_____

_____

obey His voice, and that you
may cling to Him, for He is
your life and the length of your
days; and that you may dwell
in the land which the LORD
swore to your fathers. (Deut.
30:15–16, 19–20)

Observe and obey all these
words which I command you,
that it may go well with you
and your children after you
forever. (Deut. 12:28)

Every parent I know desires that their children grow up to
love God, to trust God, and to keep God's commandments.
Every parent desires for their children to be unselfish, generous persons who love others, trust others, and desire to live in
right relationships with others. The key to these qualities in a
child's life is *unconditional love!*

Unconditional love gives your child a strong sense of wor-
thiness and value. It is on that strong foundation of knowing
that there is no end to the love that is flowing toward him that
a child is willing to risk giving his own love away freely.

- *What new insights do you have into the godly legacy God
  desires for you to give your children?*

- *In what ways are you feeling challenged in your spirit?*

FOUR

AN AWARENESS OF CAPABILITY

One of the greatest gifts you can ever give your child is to help him or her discover and develop unique talents and abilities. Every child needs to know that he or she is *capable* of doing something that is good, beneficial, or helpful. An awareness of capability is vital for emotional health and well-being.

Awareness of capability is an important foundation for a child to believe that he has something of *eternal* benefit to offer the world. Our capability in Christ Jesus includes *spiritual gifts*—those that the Holy Spirit imparts to us as permanent ministry or motivational gifts, and those the Holy Spirit imparts to us temporarily as He wills.

A child who has a strong understanding that he can contribute to the family, to society, to the church, and to the kingdom of God has purpose, focus, direction, and a greater desire to pursue and develop personal talents with enthusiasm.

- *Have you discovered your own "capabilities"? Have you discovered your child's true potential and God-given talents?*

_____

_____

- *How does it feel to know that you are "good" at something and that what you do helps others?*

_____

_____

Every Child Is "Gifted"

Every child has been gifted by God. Each person has been given permanent and resident talents, abilities, propensities, and capacities from birth.

The challenge for most parents is that a child's God-given gifts may not be the gifts the *parent* wanted his child to have. We see this in the mother who desires for her daughter to become an actress because the mother has never fulfilled her desire to be an actress, or the father who demands that his son become a better athlete than he ever was. Proverbs 22:6 is one of the most quoted and least understood verses in the Bible:

> Train up a child in the way he should go,
> And when he is old he will not depart from it.

Many parents read this verse as "train up a child in the way I, as a parent, want my child to go." The truth is that we are to train up our children in the way God has designed for them to go from their birth. Certainly that means obeying God's commandments, receiving Christ's forgiveness, and walking in righteousness—but it also means unlocking and developing the unique gifts that God has given to the child. It means developing all of the *child's* God-given abilities, not demanding that the child pursue all parent-desired opportunities!

Parents must also understand that their *spiritual* gifts and those of their child may differ. Many parents want their children to follow in their particular ministries or manifestations of spiritual gifts. God may very well have a different idea.

The goal every parent faces is to help a child discover *his or her* gifts, both natural and spiritual.

- *How do you feel about you and your child not having the same talents or gifts?*

_____

_____

- *How do you feel when you engage in an activity in which your gifts are used? How does it feel to know that you are "good" at what you do? How does it feel when you engage in activities for which you are not gifted?*

_____

_____

Unique and Wonderful Gifts

Every child should be encouraged by the good news that he or she has been given unique and wonderful gifts by a loving heavenly Father. God said about every child ever born the same thing He said repeatedly about all other aspects of His creation: "It is good." A child's gifts are *good,* and they are intended to produce good on the earth. While we human beings may prize certain gifts more than others, *God* gives gifts as *He* wills and desires, and from His perspective, all gifts and talents are good and have the seed of benefit in them.

Furthermore, no two people will function in their gifts—natural or spiritual—in precisely the same way because we each have different personalities, skills, life experiences, and emotional temperaments. Encourage your child to discover his or her unique giftedness and to express his talents in the way that is uniquely his own.

- *Can you cite an example in your life in which you and another person who seem to be gifted in the same area manifest your gifts in very different ways?*

_____

_____

What the Word Says

I will praise You, for I am fear-
fully and wonderfully made;
Marvelous are Your works,
And that my soul knows very
well.
My frame was not hidden from
You,
When I was made in secret,
And skillfully wrought in the
lowest parts of the earth.
Your eyes saw my substance,
being yet unformed.
And in Your book they all were
written,
The days fashioned for me,
When as yet there were none
of them. (Ps. 139:14–16)

I have put wisdom in the
hearts of all who are gifted
artisans, that the may make all
that I have commanded you.
(Exod. 31:6)

Behold, I have created the
blacksmith
Who blows the coals in the
fire,
Who brings forth an instru-
ment for his work. (Isa. 54:16)

Whatever your hand finds to
do, do it with your might.
(Eccles. 9:10)

What the Word Says to Me

Three Key Principles Regarding Your Child's Giftedness

There are three key principles regarding your child's giftedness:

1. *God gives us gifts but we must discover and develop them.* No person is given a full-blown gift. Every gift is given to us in the form of "potential." It is up to us to develop our gifts. How do we do that? In cooperation and in relationship with others.

The development of gifts begins with an act of faith that the Lord Jesus Christ will help us to become "doers" of the gifts that He has put within us. We only can develop our gifts—including our natural gifts—to a certain degree in our own strength. None of us has the ability within ourselves to *cause* our gifts to bless others or to be of eternal value. It is only as God infuses our gifts with *His* life that they take on eternal benefit and truly become *life*-giving.

Our challenge is to ask God to help us in the development of our gifts: to give us wise and skilled teachers, to help us develop our gifts with patience, discipline, and diligence, and to give us courage to use our gifts in relationship with other people.

Of one thing you can always assure your child—no matter what gift may be given to your child, God will *help* your child develop that gift and use it in a way that will bring glory to God's name. Every gift can become an effective tool for ministry and for soul-winning under the guidance of the Holy Spirit.

What the Word Says	What the Word Says to Me
If anyone cleanses himself . . . he will be a vessel for honor, sanctified and useful for the Master, prepared for every good work. (2 Tim. 2:21)	_____ _____ _____ _____ _____
I remind you to stir up the gift of God which is in you. (2 Tim. 1:6)	_____ _____ _____

But as God has distributed to
each one, as the Lord has
called each one, so let him
walk. (1 Cor. 7:17)

----

2. *God commands us to use our gifts as a means of serving Him and building up the Body of Christ.* The very reason we are given gifts and talents from God is so that we might use them to benefit others. While we as believers in Christ Jesus are not required to make animal sacrifices as the Israelites did in the Old Testament, we *are* called to present our own lives—our talents, time, energy, gifts—as a form of "living sacrifice" to the Lord. The Lord doesn't want only a part of us—He desires all of us to be yielded to Him and available for service to others as He inspires us to act, to speak, and to give.

What the Word Says	**What the Word Says to Me**
[Jesus said,] "I chose you and appointed you that you should go and bear fruit, and that your fruit should remain." (John 15:16)	-----------------------------------
[Jesus said,] "Abide in Me, and I in you. As the branch cannot bear fruit of itself, unless it abides in the vine, neither can you, unless you abide in Me. I am the vine, you are the branches. He who abides in Me, and I in him, bears much fruit." (John 15:4–5)	-----------------------------------

3. *God desires that we use our gifts in love, with humility, and in peace.* Only Jesus Christ embodied in physical form all spiri-

tual gifts, but each of us has been given the privilege of manifesting one *facet* of the Lord's ministry. Regardless of the gifts we have been given, we each are to manifest the *character* of Christ: love, joy, peace, longsuffering, kindness, goodness, faithfulness, gentleness, and self-control (Gal. 5:22–23). Regardless of the gifts we have been given, we are to offer them freely and with humility to other believers.

God has no tolerance for pride. A natural talent or spiritual gift should never be regarded by you or by your child as a cause for pride. Our gifts come from God, are developed as God allows us to develop them, and are of use and eternal benefit only as God provides *His* opportunities and blessing. All glory, praise, and honor that come from the exercise of our talents and gifts should always be directed to the Lord! Our praise song should be the same as that of the heavenly host:

> Blessing and glory and wisdom,
> Thanksgiving and honor and power and might,
> Be to our God forever and ever.
> Amen. (Rev. 7:12)

What the Word Says	What the Word Says to Me
Be kindly affectionate to one another with brotherly love, in honor giving preference to one another. (Rom. 12:10)	
Through love serve one another. (Gal. 5:13)	
And let the peace of God rule in your hearts, to which also you were called in one body. (Col. 3:15)	

In a very practical way, one of the greatest things we as parents can do for our children is to help them discover their aptitudes and provide lessons and mentors to help them develop their talents. Encourage your child to be diligent in practice. Provide plenty of appreciation and recognition for the talent your child is developing and the progress she is making. Recognize that your child is not going to become an expert immediately, and neither are you, in the use of his talents. Be patient and encourage a steady growth of capabilities.

Also, keep your own expectations in line as to just "how good" your child may become in a particular area of talent. Some talents are to be developed solely to give the child joy at being able to participate in a group or as a means of personally giving praise to God. Some talents are ones that may be of great blessing and benefit to other people. Recognize the difference and help your child to differentiate among his or her own talents and to discern where the greatest focus, concentration, time, and energy should be placed.

What the Word Says	What the Word Says to Me
The hand of the diligent will rule, But the lazy man will be put to forced labor. (Prov. 12:24)	----------------------------------- ----------------------------------- ----------------------------------- -----------------------------------
Diligence is man's precious possession. (Prov. 12:27)	----------------------------------- -----------------------------------
The soul of a lazy man desires, and has nothing; But the soul of the diligent shall be made rich. (Prov. 13:4)	----------------------------------- ----------------------------------- ----------------------------------- -----------------------------------
But let patience have its perfect work, that you may be	----------------------------------- ----------------------------------- -----------------------------------

perfect and complete, lacking
nothing. (James 1:4)

Whatever a man sows, that he
will also reap . . . And let us
not grow weary while doing
good, for in due season we
shall reap if we do not lose
heart. (Gal. 6:7, 9)

- *What new insights do you have into the legacy God desires
to give to your child?*

- *In what ways are you feeling challenged in your spirit today?*

FIVE

AN ABILITY TO WALK IN THE SPIRIT

Every Christian parent's greatest desire is to see their child grow up to love God and to walk daily in the Holy Spirit. As we have covered in previous lessons, the child who receives unconditional love has a strong sense of belonging to family and to the church, and the child who knows that he or she has been gifted by God is a child who develops a *predisposition* to accept God's forgiveness of sin nature and receive Christ Jesus into his life.

The predisposition to accept Christ and walk in the Spirit does not mean that a child has accepted Christ. No parent can receive Christ on behalf of a child. That is a decision that the child must make by exercising his own will.

The parent faces three challenges in teaching a child how to walk in the Spirit:

1. to lead a child to *personally* accept Christ Jesus as her Savior,
2. to learn to say no to temptation,

3. and to learn how to submit to the authority of the Holy Spirit on a daily basis.

Leading Your Child to Christ

As in all other areas of training and behavior, your child will imitate you. The more you express *your* dependence upon Jesus Christ as Savior, the more your child will want to call Him Savior. Let your child hear you thank the Lord for His forgiving you, cleansing you of your sin nature, and changing your heart so that you have a desire to follow Him and obey Him.

Also, be quick to share with your child your testimony about how *you* accepted Jesus Christ as your Savior. Your child will not think less of you for admitting that you once were a sinner.

The apostle Paul was quick to tell others what Jesus Christ had done in his life. As you read the passage below, note that Paul does not attempt to justify his former life or to make any claim that he "deserved" to be saved on his own merits:

I myself thought I must do many things contrary to the name of Jesus of Nazareth. This I also did in Jerusalem, and many of the saints I shut up in prison, having received authority from the chief priests; and when they were put to death, I cast my vote against them. And I punished them often in every synagogue and compelled them to blaspheme; and being exceedingly enraged against them, I persecuted them even to foreign cities.

While thus occupied, as I journeyed to Damascus with authority and commission from the chief priests, at midday, O king, along the road I saw a light from heaven, brighter than the sun, shining around me and those who journeyed with me. And when we all had fallen to the ground, I heard a voice speaking to me and saying in the Hebrew language, "Saul, Saul, why are you persecuting Me? It is hard for you to kick against the goads." So I said, 'Who are You, Lord?" And He said, "I am Jesus, whom you are persecuting. But rise and stand on your feet; for I have appeared to you for this purpose, to make you a minister and a witness both of the things which you have seen and of the things which I will yet reveal to you. I will deliver you from the Jewish people, as well as from the Gentiles, to whom I now send you, to open their eyes, in order to turn them from darkness to light, and from the power of Satan to God, that they may receive forgiveness of sins and an inheritance among those who are sanctified by faith in Me."

Therefore, King Agrippa, I was not disobedient to the heavenly vision. (Acts 26:9–19)

- *What is your "testimony" about how you heard and accepted Jesus Christ as your personal Savior?*

_____

_____

A second thing a parent must do is to make certain that a child knows that he must accept Jesus for himself, and how to do so. Assure your child that when she acknowledges to God that she is a sinner, God is quick to forgive.

What the Word Says	What the Word Says to Me
Jesus answered and said to him, "Most assuredly, I say to you, unless one is born of water and the Spirit, he cannot enter the kingdom of God . . . For God so loved the world that He gave His only begotten Son, that whoever believes in Him should not perish but have	

everlasting life. For God did
not send His Son into the
world to condemn the world,
but that the world through
Him might be saved." (John
3:5, 16–17)

If we confess our sins, He is
faithful and just to forgive us
our sins and to cleanse us
from all unrighteousness.
(1 John 1:9)

For "whoever calls on the
name of the LORD shall be
saved." (Rom. 10:13)

For by grace you have been
saved through faith, and that
not of yourselves; it is the gift
of God, not of works, lest anyone should boast. (Eph. 2:8–9)

A third thing a parent can do to lead a child to Christ is to
make sure the child hears the salvation message often and has
ample opportunity to respond to it. Bring your child with you
to church every Sunday, and make sure that the church you
attend preaches the message of salvation and gives an opportunity for a person to respond to the gospel and accept Christ.
Get your child involved in an active Christian youth group and
make it possible for your child to go on retreats and to camps
where the salvation message is preached as part of the overall
program.

At the same time, do not allow your child to become
involved in activities or relationships in which Christ Jesus is
ridiculed, denounced, or rejected as the Son of God. Paul

made it very clear that in the "flesh," we each have a tendency to respond to various teachings by saying "yes," "no," or "maybe" (yes and no). There are churches who also preach with these various attitudes about Christ—some preach "yes," He is the Son of God and the Savior or mankind; others preach "no," He isn't; and some preach "maybe" He is the Son of God, along with other options or qualifiers. Paul had this to say:

> The things I plan, do I plan according to the flesh, that with me there should be Yes, Yes and No, No? But as God is faithful, our word to you was not Yes and No. For the Son of God, Jesus Christ, who was preached among you by us—by me, Silvanus, and Timothy—was not Yes and No, but in Him was Yes. For all the promises of God in Him are Yes, and in Him Amen, to the glory of God through us. (2 Cor. 1:17–20)

Your responsibility as a Christian parent is *not* to give your child options about what may or may not be true, but to champion the truth about Jesus Christ as Savior. Protect your child from those influences that lead away from the gospel.

What the Word Says	What the Word Says to Me
Faith comes by hearing, and hearing by the word of God. (Rom. 10:17)	....
[Jesus said,] "I am the way, the truth, and the life. No one comes to the Father except through Me." (John 14:6)	....
[Jesus said,] "I am the door. If anyone enters by Me, he will be saved." (John 10:9)	....

Saying No to Temptation

The way your child learns to say no to temptation is to hear and see you say no to temptation. In order for us to choose good and refuse evil, we must first know what is good, true, right, and just before God. Satan presents many "counterfeits" to the believer and the unbeliever, and it is only as we know the truth that we are able to discern error.

Admit to your child that you struggle with temptation and that it is not a sin to be tempted. All people are tempted—Jesus Christ Himself was tempted by Satan! Sin occurs when we give in to temptation.

Help your child to recognize that temptation comes from the enemy of your child's soul and that the best way to defeat the enemy is the same way that Jesus defeated Satan when He was tempted: by quoting the Word of God. Help your child memorize key verses that your child might use when tempted.

And finally, assure your child that any time your child resists the devil's temptations, he can overcome the devil and that he will become stronger on the inside as a result.

Teach your child to pray any time he is faced with a temptation, "Lord Jesus, deliver me from evil. Help me to have the courage to stand for what is right." Pray that prayer with your child and for your child on a regular basis, "Lord Jesus, deliver my child from evil. Help him to have courage to stand up for what is right in every circumstance he faces today."

What the Word Says

[Jesus taught His disciples to pray,] "Do not lead us into temptation,
But deliver us from the evil one.

What the Word Says to Me

For Yours is the kingdom and the power and the glory forever. Amen." (Matt. 6:13)

Read about the temptation of Jesus in the wilderness. See Matthew 4:1–11.

Therefore submit to God. Resist the devil and he will flee from you. Draw near to God and He will draw near to you. (James 4:7–8)

Blessed is the man who endures temptation; for when he has been proved, he will receive the crown of life which the Lord has promised to those who love Him. (James 1:12)

Let no one say when he is tempted, "I am tempted by God"; for God cannot be tempted by evil, nor does He Himself tempt anyone. (James 1:13)

Walking in the Spirit

The apostle Paul wrote to the Ephesians:

Walk as children of light (for the fruit of the Spirit is in all goodness, righteousness, and truth), proving what is acceptable to the Lord. And have no fellowship with the unfruitful works of darkness, but rather expose them . . . Therefore do not be unwise, but understand what the will of the Lord is. (Eph. 5:8–11, 17)

Walking in the Spirit is a daily walk. It is trusting and relying upon the Holy Spirit every day for guidance and courage. Each of us must choose daily to be "filled" with God's Spirit so that everything we say and do is a genuine reflection of Christ Jesus in us.

Now, we need to make certain that there is no confusion about the "residency" of the Holy Spirit in us. The Holy Spirit indwells every believer at the moment he or she receives Jesus Christ as Savior. The Holy Spirit sets up permanent residence in the believer, and He does not depart. We may feel His presence more strongly at work in us at some times more than other times, but the Holy Spirit does not "leave" the believer.

To walk daily in the Holy Spirit is *to actively invite* the Holy Spirit to lead us, to guide us, to empower us, to counsel us, and to comfort us. We receive this daily work of the Holy Spirit into our lives in the same way that we received Jesus Christ as Savior—by our faith. We ask the Holy Spirit to fill us anew each morning and then believe that God is at work in us and through us all day long.

There are four vital aspects of walking in the Spirit that I believe are critical for us to teach our children:

1. *The Holy Spirit desires that each of us be separated from and cleansed of everything that is contrary to God's will for us.* In his various letters, Paul identified a number of behaviors that are contrary to the will of God for us. In most cases, Paul not only identified what we are *not* to do, but also what we *are* to do.

- "Putting away lying, each one speak truth with his neighbor" (Eph. 4:25).
- "Let all bitterness, wrath, anger, clamor, and evil speaking be put away from you, with all malice. And be kind to one another, tenderhearted, forgiving one another, just as God in Christ also forgave you" (Eph. 4:31–32).
- "But fornication and all uncleanness or covetousness, let it not even be named among you, as is fitting for saints; neither filthiness, nor foolish talking, nor coarse jesting,

which are not fitting, but rather giving of thanks" (Eph. 5:3–4).

- "Do not be drunk with wine, in which is dissipation; but be filled with the Spirit" (Eph. 5:18).

The Holy Spirit enables us not to sin, and, at the same time, the Spirit enables us to do what is right!

- *What new insights do you have into the above passages from Ephesians?*

_____

_____

What the Word Says	**What the Word Says to Me**
Therefore we were buried with Him through baptism into death, that just as Christ was raised from the dead by the glory of the Father, even so we also should walk in newness of life. (Rom. 6:4)	_____ _____ _____ _____ _____ _____ _____
Do you not know that to whom you present yourselves slaves to obey, you are that one's slaves whom you obey, whether of sin leading to death, or of obedience leading to righteousness? But God be thanked that though you were slaves of sin, yet you obeyed from the heart that form of doctrine to which you were delivered. And having been set	_____ _____ _____ _____ _____ _____ _____ _____ _____ _____ _____ _____

free from sin, you became
slaves of righteousness. (Rom.
6:16–18)

    2. *We each have a responsibility to yield ourselves entirely to Christ.* To yield oneself to the Spirit means to transfer all control over one's possessions and use of talents, time, gifts, and resources to the Holy Spirit. We must pray daily, "Holy Spirit, live Your life through me. Do not let me say or do anything that is displeasing to You today. I yield all rights of my life to You. Lead and guide me into what it is that You desire."

    In failing to yield our lives to the Holy Spirit, we are assuming responsibility for our own lives and are attempting to live in our own strength, wisdom, and power. In yielding our lives to the Spirit, we may still make mistakes because none of us is perfect in hearing from the Lord or in doing what He calls us to do, but we *can* be assured that even if we err or fall short of God's goal, the Lord will intercede on our behalf and *complete* the work He desires to do.

    Jesus taught,

> "No one can serve two masters; for either he will hate the one and love the other, or else he will be loyal to the one and despise the other. You cannot serve God and mammon." (Matt. 6:24)

    The Holy Spirit will not *demand* that we yield to Him. Yielding is a matter of our daily will.

    You as a parent can greatly influence how your child relates to the Holy Spirit by teaching your child to respect authority. You do this, in part, by showing respect for authority in your own life. Each of us is under authority to someone. The centurion who came to Jesus on behalf of his sick servant knew this (see Luke 7:1–10). Jesus Himself was under the authority of the Father. Your child is under your authority as long as you have responsibility for your child. As Paul taught, "Children, obey your parents in the Lord, for this is right" (Eph. 6:1).

Do not allow your child to be disrespectful of those in authority over him: teachers, pastors, Sunday school teachers, law-enforcement officials, or any other adult who bears responsibility for your child's welfare and who has authority in a specific jurisdiction over your child. A child who is allowed to show disrespect to parents and other adults in authority will find it very difficult to yield all authority for his life to God the Holy Spirit.

What the Word Says

[Jesus said,] "All things that I heard from My Father I have made known to you." (John 15:15)

[Jesus said,] "I honor My Father . . . And I do not seek My own glory." (John 8:49–50)

Honor your father and your mother, that your days may be long upon the land which the LORD your God is giving you. (Exod. 20:12)

Likewise you younger people, submit yourselves to your elders. Yes, all of you be submissive to one another, and be clothed with humility, for "God resists the proud, But gives grace to the humble."

What the Word Says to Me

Therefore humble yourselves
under the mighty hand of
God, that He may exalt you in
due time. (1 Peter 5:5–6)

Let this mind be in you which
was also in Christ Jesus, who,
being in the form of God, did
not consider it robbery to be
equal with God, but made
Himself of no reputation, taking the form of a servant, and
coming in the likeness of men.
And being found in appear-
ance as a man, He humbled
Himself and became obedient
to the point of death, even the
death of the cross. (Phil.
2:5–8)

3. *To be cleansed and separated from all sin and to be fully yielded
to the Holy Spirit results in a life of great joy!* To walk in the Spirit
is not to walk through life with a long face, stooped shoulders,
and a downcast expression. No! It is to walk in great exuber-
ance.

The apostle Paul encouraged the believers at Ephesus by
calling them to "be filled with the Spirit, speaking to one
another in psalms and hymns and spiritual songs, singing and
making melody in your heart to the Lord, giving thanks always
for all things to God the Father in the name of our Lord Jesus
Christ" (Eph. 5:18–20). The Christian life is intended to be a
life of great joy—knowing that we are free of sin's bondage,
guilt, and shame, and that Jesus promises us an "abundant life"
on this earth and an "eternal home with God the Father."

Let your child hear you praise God often for the direction

that the Holy Spirit is giving to your life and for the good things that you experience from His hand on a daily basis.

What the Word Says	What the Word Says to Me
These things we write to you that your joy may be full. (1 John 1:4)	
LetYour saints shout for joy. (Ps. 132:9)	
Let them shout for joy and be glad, Who favor my righteous cause; And let them say continually, "Let the LORD be magnified, Who has pleasure in the prosperity of His servant." And my tongue shall speak of Your righteousness And of Your praise all the day long." (Ps. 35:27–28)	

4. *As the Holy Spirit convicts us of sin, we must ask for immediate forgiveness.* To walk daily with the Holy Spirit means to walk in an ongoing state of cleansing and forgiveness. As the Holy Spirit brings things to our heart and mind that are not right before God, our immediate impulse must be to ask God's forgiveness. It is as we do this that we truly walk in righteousness and holiness.

What the Word Says	What the Word Says to Me
That we, having died to sins, might live for righteousness. (1 Peter 2:24)	

Grant us that we,
Being delivered from the hand
of our enemies,
Might serve Him without fear,
In holiness and righteousness
before Him all the days of our
life. (Luke 1:74–75)

Our walk in the Holy Spirit leads us into goodness and blessing. It is a joyful walk of total dependency upon the Lord that allows us to live free of sin and to experience the freedom to love God and others fully and in purity. What a great legacy a child receives if he truly comes to accept Christ Jesus as his Savior, learns to say no to temptation, and learns how to walk daily in the Spirit!

- *What new insights do you have into the legacy God desires for you to leave your children?*

- *In what ways are you feeling challenged in your spirit?*

SIX

AN ABILITY TO RELATE TO OTHERS IN A GODLY WAY

Every Christian parent has a desire for their children to "get along" with other people, and, as part of getting along, to be liked, appreciated, and respected by others. A parent gives a child a wonderful godly legacy in teaching him or her *how* to relate to other people in a way that is pleasing to God.

The apostle Paul identified a number of characteristics of the godly life and traits necessary for godly relationships. In this lesson we will focus on these aspects of the godly life:

- wholesome communication
- gentleness, kindness, and patience
- submission one to another

The principles we will cover in the first two segments relate to *all* relationships in life, those with believers in Christ Jesus and those with unbelievers. The last segment, however, has a qualifier: We are only to walk in *close fellowship* with other believers.

There are certain blessings in Christ that are reserved exclusively for those seeking to walk in the Spirit.

Does this mean that we are to live one way before nonbelievers and another before believers? No! That would be hypocrisy. We are to live as believers in Christ Jesus at all times, in all situations, regardless of circumstances or those present. The Scriptures, however, admonish us to not be "yoked" with nonbelievers. This means that we must not seek to be closely aligned with them or to be "one" with them. Those who are yoked together are like oxen pulling in the same direction for the same cause toward the same goals in life. The nonbeliever is simply not going in the same direction as the believer! We cannot truly have "unity" with those who are not following Christ. We can respect them, show kindness to them, witness to them about Christ . . . but not be in close fellowship with them.

While we are to submit to those who have authority over us, including government officials who may not be righteous, we are not to "submit" to their unrighteous ideas, which would result in our adopting those ideas as our own, or to their commands that would cause us to denounce our faith or bring disrepute upon Christ Jesus. Daniel is a great example of this. After having been carried off to Babylon along with other righteous young Jews, Daniel and his three friends, whom we know as Shadrach, Meshach, and Abed-Nego, found themselves being asked to do things that were contrary to God's laws. We have Daniel's response to this situation in Daniel 1:8:

> But Daniel purposed in his heart that he would not defile himself with the portion of the king's delicacies, nor with the wine which he drank; therefore he requested of the chief of the eunuchs that he might not defile himself.

The result of their obedience to God was that "God gave

them knowledge and skill in all literature and wisdom; and Daniel had understanding in all visions and dreams" (Dan. 1:17).

Later, when Nebuchadnezzar ordered everyone to bow down and worship a golden image he had set up, with the threat of death in a fiery furnace to all who disobeyed, Shadrach, Meshach, and Abed-Nego said this to the king:

> O Nebuchadnezzar, we have no need to answer you in this matter. If that is the case, our God whom we serve is able to deliver us from the burning fiery furnace, and He will deliver us from your hand, O king. But if not, let it be known to you, O king, that we do not serve your gods, nor will we worship the gold image which you have set up. (Dan. 3:16–18)

Any time that we do not submit to those in authority, we must be prepared to accept the consequences of our actions. Nevertheless, to submit to some people in their evil intent is to *reject God* and to fail to submit to His commandments and authority—and that is something we must never do!

- *What new insights do you have into these passages from Daniel?*

  _____

  _____

- *Have you had experiences in which you attempted to live in a "yoked" relationship with an ungodly person? What were the results?*

  _____

  _____

There are those who may think, "This sounds as if the Christian life is an exclusive life." No! All are invited by Christ Jesus to participate in His life. All are to be given an opportunity to know Him and to receive Him, and thereby, to be forgiven and reconciled to God the Father. There is no exclusivity to "membership in Christ Jesus."

Once we are in Christ Jesus, however, we *are* to walk in a way that some have come to call "the straight and narrow." Are we free to do anything we like in this life as Christians? No. We are to walk in a prescribed way of righteousness that is pleasing to God—a way that refrains from sin. Are we to think anything we want to think? No. We *are* to be narrow-minded— our minds are to be focused on those things that are edifying and that bring glory to God. There are many things that we as believers are *not* to think about, imagine, or dwell upon in our minds (see Phil. 4:8–9).

Exclusive? No. We should always be presenting the Gospel to unbelievers and inviting them to accept Christ and become part of the Body of Christ. Disciplined, focused, bonded together with those of like mind in our pursuit of a godly life? Yes!

- *How do you feel about the fact that you are not to be "yoked" with unbelievers?*

_____

_____

What the Word Says

Do not be unequally yoked together with unbelievers. For what fellowship has righteousness with lawlessness? And what communion has light with darkness? And what accord has Christ with Belial? Or what part has a believer with an unbeliever? And what agreement has the temple of

What the Word Says to Me

God with idols? . . .
Therefore
"Come out from among them
And be separate, says the
Lord.
Do not touch what is unclean,
And I will receive you."
(2 Cor. 6:14–16, 17, Isa.
52:11, and Ezek. 20:34, 41)

We give no offense in anything,
that our ministry may not be
blamed. But in all things we
commend ourselves as minis-
ters of God: in much patience,
in tribulations, in needs, in dis-
tresses . . . by purity, by
knowledge, by longsuffering,
by kindness, by the Holy
Spirit, by sincere love, by the
word of truth, by the power of
God, by the armor of righteousness on the right hand and
on the left. (2 Cor. 6:3–7)

Whatever things are true . . .
noble . . . just . . . pure . . .
lovely . . . of good report, if
there is any virtue and if there
is anything praiseworthy—med-
itate on these things. (Phil. 4:8)

Wholesome Communication

How we speak to other people very often establishes the
nature of the relationship we come to have with them. Our

words also reveal the nature of the relationship we *presently* have with another person, or which we have had in the past. The apostle Paul said this about godly communication:

> Let no corrupt communication proceed out of your mouth, but what is good for necessary edification, that it may impart grace to the hearers. And do not grieve the Holy Spirit of God, by whom you were sealed for the day of redemption. Let all bitterness, wrath, anger, clamor, and evil speaking be put away from you, with all malice. (Eph. 4:29–31)

Later in his letter to the Ephesians, Paul calls upon them to not to engage in "foolish talking, nor coarse jesting" (Eph. 5:4).

"Corrupt" words might be considered unwholesome words. They are words that are unfit, worthless, rotten, and corrupting by nature—words that cause distrust of God, disrepute of other people, and disharmony in a body of believers. They are words that ultimately hurt the speaker of them as much as the hearer of them or the object of them.

At times, it is not *what* we say that corrupts as much as *how* we speak. Words spoken in anger, derision, or bitterness cannot produce good fruit in another person's life.

- *Have you had an experience in which you felt yourself "corrupted" by what someone said to you? Have you ever had an experience in which you were so taken back by how a person spoke to you that you could not respond positively to what they said?*

When we engage in ungodly communication, we "grieve" the Holy Spirit. It is impossible to grieve someone who doesn't love you. Because the Holy Spirit loves us so much and desires so many blessings for us, He is grieved when we speak in an ungodly manner. Why? Because what we say reflects the attitude of our heart.

Jesus taught, "Out of the abundance of the heart the mouth speaks. A good man out of the good treasure of his heart brings forth good things, and an evil man out of the evil treasure brings forth evil things . . . For by your words you will be justified, and by your words you will be condemned" (Matt. 12:34–35, 37).

Godly communication is communication that "edifies" other people—builds them up, encourages them, is helpful to them. We are to speak positive, life-giving, God-honoring words to others. And we are to do so in a way that is timely, addressing the need of the moment.

Monitor your own speech—your child may very well be repeating what you are saying! Guard your tongue. Discipline your child regarding his or her speech, just as you would any other form of behavior. What we say is just as important before God as any other form of behavior!

What the Word Says	What the Word Says to Me
Set a guard, O LORD, over my mouth; Keep watch over the door of my lips. (Ps. 141:3)	------------
A soft answer turns away wrath, But a harsh word stirs up anger. The tongue of the wise uses knowledge rightly, But the mouth of fools pours forth foolishness. (Prov. 15:1–2)	------------

Let your speech always be
with grace, seasoned with salt,
that you may know how you
ought to answer each one.
(Col. 4:6)

If anyone does not stumble in
word, he is a perfect man, able
also to bridle the whole body.
Indeed, we put bits in horses'
mouths that they may obey
us, and we turn their whole
body. Look also at ships:
although they are so large and
are driven by fierce winds,
they are turned by a very
small rudder wherever the
pilot desires. Even so the
tongue is a little member and
boasts great things. (James
3:2–5)

Out of the same mouth pro-
ceed blessing and cursing. My
brethren, these things ought
not to be so. Does a spring
send forth fresh water and bit-
ter from the same opening?
(James 3:10–11)

- *How do you feel when someone speaks to you in a way that builds you up or reminds you of the goodness and love of God?*

Gentleness, Kindness, and Patience

Throughout the New Testament, we find believers in Christ called to be gentle, kind, and patient. To do so is to reflect the very nature of God! Paul wrote that "the fruit of the Spirit is love, joy, peace, *longsuffering, kindness*, goodness, faithfulness, *gentleness*, self-control" (Gal. 5:22–23, emphasis mine).

No person is born to be gentle, kind, or patient. These attributes are not part of our inborn nature. We must *learn* to be gentle, kind, and patient—and it is the responsibility of a parent to teach a child these *behavior traits* until they are automatic in a child and become *character traits*. How do we teach these behaviors? Through repeated training—insisting that a child act with gentleness, rewarding a child for kindness, and reminding a child to be patient. And, at all times, we are to treat our child with kindness, gentleness, and patience. There is no excuse from God's point of view for a parent who abuses a child, is harsh with a child, or who loses his temper with a child.

Kindness, gentleness, and patience require great discipline and self-control on the part of any person, including any child. We must ask the Lord daily to help us control our desires and impulses, and to "put them under the bridle" of the Holy Spirit.

- *How have you felt when others have treated you with gentleness, kindness, and patience? How have you felt when you have been treated harshly, unkindly, or with impatience?*

_____

_____

What the Word Says	What the Word Says to Me
Whoever has no rule over his own spirit Is like a city broken down, without walls. (Prov. 25:28)	_____ _____ _____ _____

He who is slow to anger is
better than the mighty,
And he who rules his spirit
than he who takes a city.
(Prov. 16:32)

Remind them . . . to speak evil
of no one, to be peaceable,
gentle, showing all humility to
all men. (Titus 3:1–2)

But the wisdom that is from
above is first pure, then peaceable, gentle, willing to yield,
full of mercy and good fruits,
without partiality and without
hypocrisy. (James 3:17)

Add to your faith virtue, to
virtue knowledge, to knowledge self-control, to self-
control perseverance, to perseverance godliness, to godliness
brotherly kindness, and to
brotherly kindness love. For if
these things are yours and
abound, you will be neither
barren nor unfruitful in the
knowledge of our Lord Jesus
Christ. (2 Peter 1:5–8)

Submission to One Another

Submission is rooted in two key words: *humility* and *trust*.
As believers, we are to submit to other believers *because we*

together are in Christ Jesus. We each are subject to God, and therefore we each are to be in a position of humility before God. Being humble does not mean being a "doormat." It means bowing before God in awe, respect, and worship to say, "I am your servant. I will do whatever You tell me to do." It is as we see ourselves as being a servant of God that we are able to be what Christ calls us to be—a servant to others.

Humility is not having an inferiority complex. It not saying, "I am a nobody" or "I'm not worth anything." Rather, it is saying, "I am in submission to God." The Greeks and the Romans had no use for this word *humility*—to them, it was a "slave" word. Only slaves were "humble." To the Christian, being humble was to be under the bridle of God, to be made useful and desirable from God's perspective. Humility is the attitude we see in John the Baptist—who was never a shy, retiring wimp—when he said of Jesus, "There stands One among you whom you do not know. It is He who, coming after me, is preferred before me, whose sandal strap I am not worthy to loose" (John 1:26–27).

Trust is a second key ingredient. When we submit ourselves to others, we are yielding the *authority of decision making over our life* to that other person. It is only because we truly are trusting God to work in our life, in the life of the person over us, and in the life of the person who is over them, that we ultimately are able to submit to the *decisions* that another person makes regarding our life. The believer is called to trust God—and only God—to work *all* things together for our eternal good.

Of one thing we can be assured, when we submit ourselves to others in humility and trust before God, *He* will reward us.

• *How do you feel when you hear the word* humility?

_____

_____

What the Word Says	**What the Word Says to Me**
We know that all things work together for good to those who love God, to those who are the called according to His purpose. (Rom. 8:28)	------------------------------ ------------------------------ ------------------------------ ------------------------------ ------------------------------
Remind them to be subject to rulers and authorities, to obey, to be ready for every good work. (Titus 3:1)	------------------------------ ------------------------------ ------------------------------ ------------------------------
Wives, submit to your own husbands, as is fitting in the Lord. Husbands, love your wives and do not be bitter toward them. Children, obey your parents in all things, for this is well pleasing to the Lord. Fathers, do not provoke your children, lest they become discouraged. Servants, obey in all things your masters according to the flesh, not with eyeservice, as men-pleasers, but in sincerity of heart, fearing God. And whatever you do, do it heartily, as to the Lord and not to men, knowing that from the Lord you will receive the reward of the inheritance; for you serve the Lord Christ. (Col. 3:18–24)	------------------------------ ------------------------------

In teaching our children how to communicate in a godly way with others, how to treat others with gentleness, kindness, and patience, and how to submit to others in ways that are pleasing to God, we are preparing our children not only to lead godly lives, but how to establish godly homes, godly business partnerships, and godly communities. What a wonderful legacy to be taught *how* to have good relationships! The person who treats others in a godly way is a person who is respected and admired, even in times of disagreement.

- *What new insights do you have into the godly legacy the Lord desires for you to leave your children?*

_____

_____

- *In what ways are you feeling challenged in your spirit?*

_____

_____

SEVEN

A GROWING RELATIONSHIP WITH THE LORD

The greatest inheritance you can ever leave your child is a spiritual inheritance—salvation and the assurance of a heavenly home, followed by a desire and an understanding about what it means to *grow* in one's relationship with the Lord.

Our salvation is secured by believing in the Lord Jesus Christ as Savior and receiving the forgiveness that God the Father makes available through Him. No other actions or deeds are required. As Jesus said,

> "This is the work of God, that you believe in Him whom He sent . . . And this is the will of Him who sent Me, that everyone who sees the Son and believes in Him may have everlasting life; and I will raise him up at the last day." (John 6:29, 40)

Salvation is the step that *establishes* the most important relationship your child will ever know—a relationship with God Almighty. It is, however, only the first step in that relationship. Our relationship with the Lord is expected to become richer, deeper, and more intimate every day from the day of our salvation to the day we die.

How does that happen? Through prayer and by spending time with the Lord, listening to what He says to us. *Teach* your child to pray.

How a Child Learns to Pray

A child learns to pray in this way:

1. *A child hears and mimics the way his parents pray—in both terminology and attitude.*

If you don't pray with and for your child, allowing your child to hear you voice spontaneous personal prayers, your child isn't going to pray. He is going to expect prayer only from a pastor's lips in a church setting. On the other hand, if you are quick to pray—any time, any place, about anything—your child will come to see that prayer is a normal part of everyday life, and he will be quick to pray.

Your child will pray the way *you* pray—he will copy your words, your phrases, and your posture as you pray.

> • *What has been your experience with prayer? How did you learn to pray? Who is it that you "mimic" when you pray—who was your "prayer teacher"?*

_____

_____

In addition, your child will copy your attitude toward God as you pray. Children are quick to pick up the attitudes and emotions of the adults around them. What you say to God is going to be interpreted by your child to a great extent by how you say what you say.

If your attitude is that God is a harsh judge just waiting to pronounce punishment upon you, your child will pick up on that attitude and approach God the same way you do, with fear and caution.

On the other hand, if your attitude is that God is a loving heavenly Father who is delighted at the opportunity to bless, guide, and help His children, your child will approach God with the same attitude—one generally marked by joy, vulnerability, and familiarity.

If you consider prayer a *duty* and an obligation, your child will regard prayer the same way. If you approach prayer as a *delight* and a privilege, your child will approach times of prayer eagerly and expectantly.

If you don't truly know God yourself and see Him as being distant and uninvolved in your personal life, your child will approach God as a stranger. If you have developed an intimate relationship with God, your child will approach God as Friend.

If you pray with stilted, formal language, your child will come to regard prayer as a formal occasion. If you pray in everyday language, your child will be quick to pray in his own childlike terms.

- *What is your attitude—what are your emotions—as you pray?*

_____

_____

2. *What you pray for will be what your child prays for.* If you only pray about great, important things or in crisis times, your child is likely to pray only about major events, desires, and problems in his life. If you pray about virtually *everything*, your child is going to regard prayer as a normal, ongoing conversation with God. Your child will come to believe he or she can talk to God about *anything*.

Encourage your child to pray for his daily needs. A child who sees God as the Provider of all good things is a child who can trust God in all situations to do what is right, good, and beneficial.

Especially encourage your child to pray for a daily forgiveness of his or her sins. A child who believes that God forgives freely—and frequently—is a child who lives in freedom from abiding guilt and shame. Such a child is much more quick to receive the Lord Jesus as Savior and to invite the Holy Spirit to come into her life and transform his very desire to sin into a desire to obey God. Encourage your child also to forgive others and to pray especially for those who may be persecuting him.

Also encourage your child to pray specifically for those in positions of leadership and authority, and to pray for pastors, missionaries, and all who proclaim the gospel of Jesus Christ, as well as for Christians in other countries who are going through times of persecution. In praying for other believers, your child will have a growing awareness of the Body of Christ around the world and have a growing compassion for lost souls.

What the Word Says	What the Word Says to Me
[Jesus said,] "Give us this day our daily bread." (Matt. 6:11)	--
[Jesus said,] "Forgive us our debts, As we forgive our debtors." (Matt. 6:12)	--
[Jesus said,] "Pray for those who spitefully use you." (Luke 6:28)	--
For we do not want you to be ignorant, brethren, of our trouble which came to us in Asia: that we were burdened beyond measure, above strength, so	--

that we despaired even of life.
Yes, we had the sentence of
death in ourselves, that we
should not trust in ourselves but
in God who raises the dead,
who delivered us from so great a
death, and does deliver us; in
whom we trust that He will still
deliver us, *you also helping*
together in prayer for us, that
thanks may be given by many
persons on our behalf for the
gift granted to us through many.
(2 Cor. 1:8–11, emphasis mine)

Therefore I exhort first of all
that supplications, prayers,
intercessions, and giving of
thanks be made for all men,
for kings and all who are in
authority, that we may lead a
quiet and peaceable life in all
godliness and reverence.
(1 Tim. 2:1–2)

3. *What your child hears you pray* on his behalf *will have great impact on your child's life.* If your prayers are vague on your child's behalf—"Oh God, bless little Johnny, be with little Mary today"—your child is going to have fairly vague feelings about God's involvement in his life.

On the other hand, if your prayers are specific—"Father, help Johnny with his math test today, give him a clear mind and an ability to concentrate and do his best, and give Mary the courage to smile and walk boldly when unkind children tease her"—your child is going to see God as being actively involved and of personal help every hour of his day.

A child who is sent off to school or to play every morning with prayer on his behalf is a child who is going to be much better equipped to withstand temptation, have courage in the face of difficulty, feel confident in the love of God, and be quicker to act on what is right in God's eyes.

One of the greatest "teachers" about prayer in the New Testament was the apostle Paul. He taught *by example*. He opens several of his letters with prayers. As you read through a few of these below, think how it must have felt for the early Christian believers to receive these letters and to hear what Paul was praying on their behalf. How encouraging his words would have been to them—and are to us today!

What the Word Says	**What the Word Says to Me**
I thank my God upon every remembrance of you, always in every prayer of mine making request for you all with joy, for your fellowship in the gospel from the first day until now, being confident of this very thing, that He who has begun a good work in you will complete it until the day of Jesus Christ. (Phil. 1:3–6)	_____ _____ _____ _____ _____ _____ _____ _____ _____ _____
For this reason we also . . . do not cease to pray for you, and to ask that you may be filled with the knowledge of His will in all wisdom and spiritual understanding; that you may have a walk worthy of the	_____ _____ _____ _____ _____ _____ _____

Lord, fully pleasing Him, being
fruitful in every good work and
increasing in the knowledge of
God; strengthened with all
might, according to His glori-
ous power, for all patience and
longsuffering with joy; giving
thanks to the Father who has
qualified us to be partakers of
the inheritance of the saints in
the light. (Col. 1:9–12)

4. *A child whose prayers are invited and welcomed by a parent is a child who begins to grow in his own relationship with God.* Pray *with* your child. Invite your child to voice his or her own petitions to God and to pray about whatever he desires, whenever he feels a need to pray. Never criticize the words your child uses in prayer. Allow your child free expression before God—after all, God looks on the heart, not at vocabulary.

Ask your child to pray about specific needs in your family and, from time to time, to pray for you about specific issues you are facing or problems that you have. This is not to say that you should burden your child with all the details of your troubles, frighten your child, or make your child feel responsible for your problems. Rather, it is to *invite* your child to participate more fully in your life and to build a relationship "in the Spirit" with your child. Such a relationship is highly valued by a child and especially so as your child becomes a parent himself one day.

Encourage your child in the fact that he has been given faith by God (Rom. 12:3). Teach your child to pray with *faith* that God hears prayers, answers prayers, and that God will uses our prayers to bring about an eternal benefit in his life and in the lives of others.

Furthermore, in inviting your child to pray for you and for

others in your family, you are expressing in a very powerful way that you love your child and that he belongs to your family. You are expressing appreciation for your child's *spiritual* nature and your belief that God desires an ever-growing relationship with your child.

You may ask, "When is a child old enough to pray for himself or to pray for other people?" As soon as your child can talk!

"But what," you may say, "if God does not answer my child's prayer. How can I explain that?"

God always answers the prayer of a sincere heart—He just may not answer in the way we *want* Him to answer. God's answers to us are "yes," "no," "not at this time," and "if certain conditions are met." Teach your child that a "no" answer from God is still an answer, and that it is the *best* answer at this time from a loving heavenly Father, even if we don't understand why He has said "no" to us on a particular matter.

Teach your child about the power of agreement in prayer—that if any two believers in Christ Jesus ask something of our heavenly Father, He will hear and answer their prayer according to His will, which is always for our eternal benefit (see Matt. 18:19–20).

What the Word Says	What the Word Says to Me
Pray for us. (Heb. 13:18)	---
God has dealt to each one a measure of faith. (Rom. 12:3)	--- ---
[Jesus said,] "Again I say to you that if two of you agree on earth concerning anything that they ask, it will be done for them by My Father in heaven. For where two or three are gathered together in My name,	--- --- --- --- --- --- ---

I am there in the midst of
them." (Matt. 18:19–20)

Let him ask in faith, with no
doubting, for he who doubts is
like a wave of the sea driven
and tossed by the wind. (James
1:6)

[Jesus said,] "Whatever you
ask in My name, that I will do,
that the Father may be glori-
fied in the Son. If you ask
anything in My name, I will do
it." (John 14:13–14)

Praise and Thanksgiving

Always throughout the Scriptures, we are encouraged to
approach God with praise and thanksgiving. Praise and thanksgiving are to become the foundational attitude of our lives as
believers in Christ Jesus. The person with an attitude of praise
and thanksgiving stands in humility before God, quick to
acknowledge "I cannot, but You, God, can do all things." To
have an attitude of praise and thanksgiving to God is to
develop an attitude of gratitude and appreciation for all that a
person is given. What a wonderful legacy it is for a child to
regard all of life as a "gift" from a loving Father—a gift to be
cherished, used wisely, and enjoyed fully.

Every prayer we voice should begin and end with thanksgiving and praise. When Jesus taught His disciples to pray, He
taught them to begin their prayer with praise:

"Our Father in heaven,
Hallowed be Your name." (Matt. 6:9)

Jesus also taught them to end their prayer with praise:

"For Yours is the kingdom and the power and the glory forever." (Matt. 6:13)

Let your child hear you voice praise and thanksgiving often, every day. Praise God for the little things as well as the big things. Praise God not only for what He has done but for who He is—our loving, merciful, forgiving heavenly Father who delights in being our Provider, Sustainer, Deliverer, Counselor, Help, Friend, and Protector.

When we praise and thank God, we open our lives to Him in a way that allows us to receive even more of His blessings and to experience even more joy in His presence. The more praise and thanksgiving we voice with our prayers, the greater the peace and assurance we have that God *will* act on our behalf.

• *How do you feel after you have spent time praising and thanking God for His many blessings?*

_____

_____

What the Word Says

By prayer and supplication, with thanksgiving, let your requests be made known to God; and the peace of God, which surpasses all under-standing, will guard your hearts and minds through Christ Jesus. (Phil. 4:6–7)

Enter into His gates with thanksgiving,
And into His courts with praise.

What the Word Says to Me

Be thankful to Him, and bless
His name.
For the LORD is good;
His mercy is everlasting,
And His truth endures to all
generations. (Ps. 100:4–5)

Developing a Listening Heart

In addition to voicing petitions and praise and thanksgiving to God, encourage your child to spend time listening to God. God speaks continually to His people, but those who truly are listening for His voice are those who tend to hear what He says to them. God speaks in a still, small voice to our hearts, and it is up to each of us to open our spiritual ears and listen intently. Every time you read the Bible with your child, begin your time with prayer, inviting the Holy Spirit to speak to your hearts the truth of God's Word and to help you understand the message God has for you to hear.

Encourage your child that God speaks words of encouragement and edification to the heart. God causes us to feel convicted about our sins—not so that we might fear punishment, but so that we might ask for God's forgiveness. Above all, God speaks to us of His great love for us.

What a wonderful legacy it is for your child to learn to hear from God for himself—to trust in God, to turn quickly to God in every situation, to receive God's assurance and love, and to know without doubt that God is present with him always!

What the Word Says

And the LORD called Samuel again the third time. Then he arose and went to Eli, and said, "Here I am, for you did call me." Then Eli perceived

What the Word Says to Me

----

that the LORD had called the
boy. Therefore Eli said to
Samuel, "Go, lie down; and it
shall be, if He calls you, that
you must say, 'Speak, LORD,
for Your servant hears.'" So
Samuel went and lay down in
his place. Then the LORD came
and stood and called as at
other times, "Samuel!
Samuel!" And Samuel
answered, "Speak, for Your servant hears." (1 Sam. 3:8–10)

My soul, wait silently for God
alone,
For my expectation is from
Him. (Ps. 62:5)

- *What new insights do you have into the legacy God desires for you to give your children?*

_____

_____

- *In what ways are you feeling challenged in your spirit?*

_____

_____

EIGHT

A HIGH VALUE UPON GOD'S WORD

If you were able to give your child the *best*, most beneficial, and wisest advice in the world—at all times throughout his or her life—you would no doubt feel that you were an excellent parent. The fact is, you *can* give your child such advice by teaching your child to read the Bible and to turn *first* to the Bible for answers to life's problems, needs, and questions.

Repeatedly, the Scriptures command us as parents to *teach* God's Word to our children. This is not the sole responsibility of a pastor or a Sunday school teacher. It is every parent's responsibility to make certain his or her child knows God's Word:

> Hear, O Israel: The LORD our God, the LORD is one! You shall love the LORD your God with all your heart, with all your soul, and with all your might. And these words which I command you today shall be in your heart. You shall teach them diligently to your children, and shall talk of them when you sit in your house, when you walk by the way, when you lie down, and when you rise up. You shall bind them as a sign on your hand, and

they shall be as frontlets between your eyes. You shall write them on the doorposts of your house and on your gates. (Deut. 6:4–9)

The Word of God is to become the very perspective or attitude of our lives—we are to see the world through the lens of God's Word. God's truth is to be the motivation for all we do—everything we say and do should become a reflection of God's Word. God's truth is to reign supreme in our homes. Anyone who is around our family should recognize that God's truth is the "law" for our family, the rule we live by, and the code of conduct we strive to uphold.

Furthermore, we are to teach God's Word in a natural way to our children—morning to night, as we talk about things we encounter and as we reflect upon various situations and circumstances in our lives.

God's Word is a spiritual document, and it is learned in the *spirit* of your child. God's Word must become the foundation on which your child's *conscience* is built. It must be to your child the "right way" to live and to believe.

- *In your experience, how did you learn right from wrong? On what was your understanding of right and wrong based?*

_____

_____

- *In your experience, what happens when a person does not know the truth of God's Word and has no real understanding of right and wrong?*

_____

_____

What the Word Says

Therefore you shall love the LORD your God, and keep His

What the Word Says to Me

----

charge, His statutes, His judgments, and His commandments
always. (Deut. 11:1)

What does the LORD your God
require of you, but to fear the
LORD your God, to walk in all
His ways and to love Him, to
serve the LORD your God with
all your heart and with all your
soul, and to keep the commandments of the LORD and
His statutes which I command
you today for your good?
(Deut. 10:12–13)

[Jesus said,] "If anyone loves
Me, he will keep My word; and
My Father will love him, and
We will come to him and make
Our home with him. He who
does not love Me does not
keep My words; and the word
which you hear is not Mine
but the Father's who sent Me."
(John 14:23–24)

[Jesus said,] "If you abide in
Me, and My words abide in
you, you will ask what you
desire, and it shall be done for
you." (John 15:7)

• *What new insights do you have about the importance of leaving a love for God's Word as a legacy to your children?*

_____

_____

How a Child Learns God's Word

A child learns God's Word in three important ways:

1. *Your child learns God's Word and begins to appreciate it through your reading God's Word aloud.* Reading gives a child an awareness of language, broadens a child's horizons, creates a child's love for learning, and gives a child a feeling of closeness to the parent who is reading to him. When a parent reads God's Word—usually in the form of Bible stories at the beginning of a child's life—that parent builds into a child all of the benefits of reading with these added advantages: an awareness of God's presence, an understanding about how God works and why we must obey God, and a feeling of closeness to God.

Always uphold to your child the *importance* of God's Word— that it is the truth of God, the way we are to live, and that it is for our benefit now and forever. The Bible is not "just another story"—it is *the* book of books.

What the Word Says	What the Word Says to Me
My son, keep my words,	-----------------------------------
And treasure my commands	-----------------------------------
within you.	-----------------------------------
Keep my commands and live,	-----------------------------------
And my law as the apple of	-----------------------------------
your eye.	-----------------------------------
Bind them on your fingers;	-----------------------------------
Write them on the tablet of	-----------------------------------
your heart.	-----------------------------------
Say to wisdom, "You are my	-----------------------------------
sister,"	-----------------------------------
And call understanding your	-----------------------------------

nearest kin. (Prov. 7:1–4)

The fear of the LORD is the
beginning of wisdom,
And the knowledge of the
Holy One is understanding.
(Prov. 9:10)

2. *The second way your child learns God's Word is by memorizing Scripture.* Even when your child may not understand all of the vocabulary words or the full meaning of a verse, a child *can* memorize God's Word. When the Word is hidden away in a child's lasting memory, the Holy Spirit can bring God's truth to remembrance at precisely the time it is needed most. What a child hasn't learned, the Holy Spirit cannot recall!

When your child memorizes God's Word he also establishes the truth of God as part of the very way he *thinks* and, therefore, acts. When the truth of God becomes the *first* or *foundational* way that a child thinks, that child will always have a God-first, what-God-says-matters perspective on life.

What the Word Says	What the Word Says to Me
My son, if you receive my words,	
And treasure my commands within you,	
So that you incline your ear to wisdom,	
And apply your heart to understanding;	
Yes, if you cry out for discernment,	
And lift up your voice for understanding,	
If you seek her as silver,	

And search for her as hidden
treasures;
Then you will understand the
fear of the LORD,
And find the knowledge of God.
For the LORD gives wisdom;
From His mouth come knowl-
edge and understanding;
He stores up sound wisdom
for the upright;
He is a shield to those who
walk uprightly;
He guards the paths of justice,
And preserves the way of His
saints.
Then you will understand
righteousness and justice,
Equity and every good path.
(Prov. 2:1–9)

3. *A child learns God's Word by reading and studying God's
Word.* As soon as your child is able to read, encourage the reading of God's Word. Buy a translation of the Bible your child
can understand. Many Bibles have study notes for children and
young adults.

Encourage your child to go to the Bible to discover answers
to questions about life. Show your child how to use a concor-
dance, a Bible dictionary, and various other Bible-study helps.
Actively explore—*together*—the Bible's answers to specific
problems or needs your child faces.

The more your child sees the Bible as applicable and beneficial to his or her own life, the quicker he will be to turn to
the Bible for God's answers.

Your child will benefit greatly from seeing *you* reading the
Bible often and by seeing *you* go to the Bible for answers in

your own life. A love of God's Word comes to your child as she sees you valuing God's Word!

What the Word Says	What the Word Says to Me
Study to shew thyself approved unto God, a workman that needeth not to be ashamed, rightly dividing the word of truth. But shun profane and vain babblings: for they will increase unto more ungodliness. (2 Tim. 2:15–16 KJV)	--
All Scripture is given by inspiration of God, and is profitable for doctrine, for reproof, for correction, for instruction in righteousness, that the man of God may be complete, thoroughly equipped for every good work. (2 Tim. 3:16–17)	--
Through Your precepts I get understanding; Therefore I hate every false way. Your word is a lamp to my feet And a light to my path. (Ps. 119:104–105)	--

Believe What You Read!

Children encounter a great deal in our world today that is imaginary or mythical. Encourage your child always to approach God's Word as lasting, eternal, rock-solid truth.

The Bible presents what is pleasing and desired by God—it tells how to relate to God, how to relate to others, and how to have peace of heart. It is the key to all understanding about human nature, God's nature, and about spiritual reality.

God does not desire that we live in a state of confusion or darkness. The very opposite is true! He desires that we walk in wisdom, knowing what is good, right, and helpful. We are to know truth, to walk in truth, and to speak truth!

What the Word Says	What the Word Says to Me
For this reason we also thank God without ceasing, because when you received the word of God which you heard from us, you welcomed it not as the word of men, but as it is in truth, the word of God, which also effectively works in you who believe. (1 Thess. 2:13)	
The entirety of Your word is truth, And every one of Your righteous judgments endures forever. (Ps. 119:160)	
Great peace have those who love Your law, And nothing causes them to stumble. (Ps. 119:165)	
[Jesus prayed for His followers,] "Sanctify them by Your truth. Your word is truth." (John 17:17)	

Furthermore, God expects us to act upon what we read. We are to *do* God's Word—live out His truth, express His message to others, and be witnesses to the gospel of Jesus Christ. We are to live what we believe. We are not called simply to "talk the talk" of God's Word, but to "walk the walk."

What the Word Says	What the Word Says to Me
Be doers of the word, and not hearers only, deceiving yourselves. (James 1:22)	
He who keeps instruction is in the way of life, But he who refuses reproof goes astray. (Prov. 10:17)	

Finally, God's Word has been given to us for our benefit. His Word is *life*-giving—it produces in us an awareness about how we can receive eternal life through God's Son, and it creates in us the capacity to recognize God's blessings and a desire to receive them. God's commandments are not given to us to "take away our fun" or to put us in a spiritual straitjacket, but rather, they are given to us for our protection and so we might be in a position to receive all of the good things God desires for us. Encourage your child not only to believe what the Word says and to do what the Word commands, but to look for the blessing that comes from believing and obeying God's Word!

What the Word Says	What the Word Says to Me
And the LORD commanded us to observe all these statutes, to fear the LORD our God, for our good always, that He might preserve us alive, as it is this	

day. Then it will be righteousness for us, if we are careful to
observe all these commandments before the LORD our
God, as He has commanded
us. (Deut. 6:24–25)

You shall walk in all the ways
which the LORD your God has
commanded you, that you may
live and that it may be well
with you, and that you may
prolong your days in the land
which you shall possess. (Deut.
5:33)

A child who knows where to go for answers in times of doubt, trouble, or need for problem-solving and decision-making advice, and who learns to read and understand God's Word independently is always going to have access to wise counsel!

- *What new insights do you have into the legacy God desires for you to leave your child?*

_____

_____

- *In what ways are you feeling challenged in your spirit today?*

_____

_____

NINE

FACING AND OVERCOMING PROBLEMS AND UNPLEASANT SITUATIONS

Christians are not immune from problems, trials, and troubles. We each encounter unpleasant situations and circumstances from time to time in our lives. One of the greatest gifts any parent can give a child is an ability to recognize the true source of all problems, to face problems squarely in the power of the Holy Spirit, and to overcome problems.

The world in which the apostle Paul lived was filled with problems and unpleasant situations. The majority of people in his day were slaves living in cities and regions that had been occupied by Rome. Thus, the majority of the people in the first churches to which Paul wrote were slaves. Paul himself was never a slave to a human master. However, he frequently referred to himself as a bondservant of Jesus Christ—he saw himself as being in total submission to, and his life ruled by Jesus Christ, his master and lord.

While Paul never taught that a person should *like* being a slave, he did teach that a person can be "content" in whatever state he finds himself and that, on the inside and in the Spirit, a believer in Christ Jesus can live as a "free person" (see 1 Peter 2:15–16).

It is Paul's teaching for how to live victoriously in unpleasant and problematic situations that is at the heart of this lesson.

- *Identify an experience you have had that was unpleasant or problematic to you. How did Christ Jesus call upon you to respond to that experience?*

_____

_____

While you can promise your child that those who believe in Christ Jesus will live forever and happily with the Lord . . . never promise your child that he will grow up to live "happily ever after" in this lifetime.

While you can promise your child that God has great blessings for him in his future . . . never promise your child that he will live a life free of problems and struggles.

While you can promise your child that God will meet all of his *needs* according to the riches of Christ Jesus . . . never promise your child that God is going to give him everything he *wants*.

Life has ups and downs—good times and bad times. To be taught otherwise is to live in fantasy. The good news to us as believers is that we always have within us the Holy Spirit to *help* us in our times of trouble, we always have the hope of heaven before us, and therefore, we can always *choose* to have a joyful attitude, no matter how difficult, painful, hurtful, unpleasant, or stressful a situation may be.

What the Word Says	What the Word Says to Me
[Jesus taught about God the Father,] "He makes His sun rise on the evil and on the good, and sends rain on the just and on the unjust." (Matt. 5:45)	--
[Jesus said,] "In the world you will have tribulation; but be of good cheer, I have overcome the world." (John 16:33)	--
I have learned in whatever state I am, to be content: I know how to be abased, and I know how to abound. Everywhere and in all things I have learned both to be full and to be hungry, both to abound and to suffer need. I can do all things through Christ who strengthens me. (Phil. 4:11–13)	--
[Jesus said,] "Therefore you now have sorrow; but I will see you again and your heart will rejoice, and your joy no one will take from you." (John 16:22)	--

Two Key Principles for Overcoming the Unpleasant

Paul placed emphasis on two key principles in overcoming the unpleasant: obedience and diligence.

1. *We are always to remain obedient to God and to those He has placed in authority over us, even in unpleasant situations.* Paul wrote this to the slaves in the church at Ephesus:

> Servants, be obedient to those who are your masters according to the flesh, with fear and trembling, in sincerity of heart, as to Christ; not with eyeservice, as men-pleasers, but as servants of Christ, doing the will of God from the heart, with good will doing service, as to the Lord, and not to men, knowing that whatever good anyone does, he will receive the same from the Lord, whether he is a slave or free. (Eph. 6:5–8)

There is no substitute for *doing* what is required of us. We are not to *say* we will fulfill an obligation only if it "suits us" at the time to keep our word. We are to *do* what we commit ourselves to do and to obey those who require service of us. Children are required to obey their parents, servants are required to obey their masters, and all of us are to obey those in spiritual and political authority over us with this attitude: *as to the Lord.* In other words, we are to obey as if God Himself is in charge of our lives—which truly is the case!

Jesus gave an illustration of the importance of our obedience, teaching,

> "A man had two sons, and he came to the first and said, 'Son, go, work today in my vineyard.' He answered and said, 'I will not,' but afterward he regretted it and went. Then he came to the second and said likewise. And he answered and said, 'I go, sir,' but he did not go. Which of the two did the will of his father?"
> They said to Him, "The first." (Matt. 21:28–31)

Obedience puts us into a position to receive God's help and God's reward. In good times and bad, we must obey what God has commanded, regardless of how we "feel" or others behave.

• *What new insights do you have into these passages from Ephesians and Matthew?*

_____

_____

2. *We are to be diligent in our work and in our witness for Christ, even in difficult or unpleasant situations.* Being diligent first means being *willing* to work hard. Often when people are faced with an unpleasant task or a difficult situation, they behave in one of these three ways: they avoid the situation as much as possible, they complain bitterly about the situation, or they do the minimal effort required in hopes of getting through the situation as quickly as possible. The Bible presents a different approach: work as if you are being paid or rewarded twice—once by the "owner" or the person in authority over you, and once by God! There is no justification for doing halfhearted work or for producing poor quality workmanship.

God sees what we do, even if nobody else does, and He sees and rewards not only what we do but our attitude while doing it.

What the Word Says	What the Word Says to Me
Then [Moses] took the Book of the Covenant and read in the hearing of the people. And they said, "All that the LORD has said we will do, and be obedient." (Exod. 24:7)	_____ _____ _____ _____ _____ _____
Then they said to Jeremiah, "Let the LORD be a true and faithful witness between us, if we do not do according to everything which the LORD your God	_____ _____ _____ _____

sends us by you. Whether it is pleasing or displeasing, we will obey the voice of the LORD . . . that it may be well with us when we obey the voice of the LORD our God." (Jer. 42:5–6)

Exhort servants to be obedient to their own masters, to be well pleasing in all things, not answering back, not pilfering, but showing all good fidelity, that they may adorn the doctrine of God our Savior in all things. (Titus 2:9–10)

Remind them to be subject to rulers and authorities, to obey, to be ready for every good work, to speak evil of no one, to be peaceable, gentle, showing all humility to all men. (Titus 3:1–2)

Whatever you do in word or deed, do all in the name of the Lord Jesus, giving thanks to God the Father through Him. (Col. 3:17)

A reward is held out to all who obey and are diligent in the face of unpleasant tasks or commandments that aren't personally to our liking. Jesus said that those who are faithful over little will be given much to rule over in the future. Those who are obedient are also those about whom the Lord feels joy. If you truly want to delight the heart of God, obey Him! (see Matt. 25:23).

What does this mean to us as parents? It means that we are to *require* obedience from our children and to refuse to accept or wink at their disobedience. We are to require that our children give full effort to the things they undertake and that they do so with a cheerful attitude all the way to the completion of the task they have started—even if that task has unpleasant aspects or results in a few difficult moments.

Parents must

- *discipline their children with love.* In this, they teach a child respect for others, respect for themselves, and ultimately respect for God.
- *be consistent in what they require of a child.* As so, they teach a child what it means to be steadfast and faithful.
- *only require of their children what God requires.* At no time are we as parents to put a burden on our child that is beyond what God requires solely for our own convenience or ego gratification.

What the Word Says	What the Word Says to Me
And you, fathers, do not provoke your children to wrath, but bring them up in the training and admonition of the Lord. (Eph. 6:4)	_____
Fathers, do not provoke your children, lest they become discouraged. (Col. 3:21)	_____
Chasten your son while there is hope, And do not set your heart on his destruction. (Prov. 19:18)	_____

Problem Versus Unpleasant

We also are to teach our children the difference between a problem and something that is uncomfortable or unpleasant. Sin and evil are the source of all problems. The unjust persecution of God's people is also a "problem" in God's eyes.

The Solution to Sin-Related Problems.

The solution for problems that arise from our personal sin is confession of our sin to God, and repentance, which is a change of our heart and our behavior. If we have hurt others by what we have said or done against them, we are also to ask their forgiveness and to make amends as best we can.

What the Word Says	What the Word Says to Me
I acknowledged my sin to You, And my iniquity I have not hidden. I said, "I will confess my transgressions to the LORD," And You forgave the iniquity of my sin. (Ps. 32:5)	....
Thus says the Lord GOD: "Repent, turn away from your idols, and turn your faces away from all your abominations." (Ezek. 14:6)	....
[Jesus said,] "Repent, and believe in the gospel." (Mark 1:15)	....
[Paul declared] . . . that they should repent, turn to God, and do works befitting repentance. (Acts 26:20)	....

The Solution to Persecution-Related Problems.

When your child is being treated unfairly by others or is suffering from "persecution," the solution lies in prayer, trusting God, and doing good to the persecutor.

First, we are to pray that God will deliver us from those who persecute us (see Ps. 142:6).

Second, we are to leave any vengeance or acts of retaliation up to God (see Rom. 12:19). Those who persecute us become "enemies" of the Lord, and to be an enemy of the Lord is to be in a very undesirable position! (see Deut. 32:43 and Nahum 1:2).

Third, we are to continue to act in a positive way toward those who persecute us until God delivers us from our persecutors. Read what Jesus said about dealing with our persecutors:

> "But I say to you, love your enemies, bless those who curse you, do good to those who hate you, and pray for those who spitefully use you and persecute you, that you may be sons of your Father in heaven." (Matt. 5:44–45)

Finally, recognize and teach your child that persecution related to faith in Jesus Christ is inevitable. Prepare your child for such persecution, which may come in the form of rejection, ridicule, teasing, or bullying. Encourage your child that his endurance of any persecution related to his faith results in a great reward from God. Jesus taught,

> "Blessed are those who are persecuted for righteousness' sake,
> For theirs is the kingdom of heaven." (Matt. 5:10)

What the Word Says	What the Word Says to Me
Attend to my cry,	---
For I am brought very low;	---
Deliver me from my persecu-	---
tors,	---

For they are stronger than I.
(Ps. 142:6)

Beloved, do not avenge yourselves, but rather give place to
wrath; for it is written,
"Vengeance is Mine, I will
repay," says the Lord.
"Therefore if your enemy
hungers, feed him;
If he thirsts, give him a drink;
For in so doing you will heap
coals of fire on his head."
Do not be overcome by evil,
but overcome evil with good.
(Rom. 12:19–21)

Rejoice, O Gentiles, with His
people;
For He will avenge the blood
of His servants,
And render vengeance to His
adversaries;
He will provide atonement for
His land and His people.
(Deut. 32:43)

God is jealous, and the LORD
avenges;
The LORD avenges and is furi-
ous.
The LORD will take vengeance
on His adversaries,
And He reserves wrath for His
enemies;

The LORD is slow to anger and
great in power,
And will not at all acquit the
wicked. (Nahum. 1:2–3)

The Solution for Satan-Created Problems.

In addition to the problems created by our own sin and by our persecutors, there are problems directly created by Satan. Satan works through persecutors and through evil people to create negative situations in our lives. We must be quick to recognize that a person who is hurting us is *not* the real source of the problem—Satan is the source. These spiritual problems are intended to destroy us and demolish our witness for Christ. The solution, spiritual warfare, is described by Paul in Ephesians 6:10–13:

> Finally, my brethren, be strong in the Lord and in the power of His might. Put on the whole armor of God, that you may be able to stand against the wiles of the devil. For we do not wrestle against flesh and blood, but against principalities, against powers, against the rulers of the darkness of this age, against spiritual hosts of wickedness in the heavenly places. Therefore take up the whole armor of God, that you may be able to withstand in the evil day, and having done all, to stand.

Paul's description of the whole armor of God is a wonderful picture of Christ in us. The armor that we are putting on is the very nature of Christ Jesus. He is our truth, our righteousness, our peace, the source of our faith, the author of our salvation, and the living Word spoken by God.

> Stand therefore, having girded your waist with truth, having put on the breastplate of righteousness, and having shod your feet with the preparation of the gospel of peace; above all, taking the shield of faith with which

you will be able to quench all the fiery darts of the
wicked one. And take the helmet of salvation, and the
sword of the Spirit, which is the word of God. (Eph.
6:14–17)

What is it that we do once we have put on the armor of God,
the nature of Christ Jesus? We are to *stand*—to endure, to
refuse to be moved from our position of righteousness, to
refuse to give in to temptation—and we are to *pray*. Paul's conclusion to putting on the whole armor is this: "praying always
with all prayer and supplication in the Spirit, being watchful
to this end with all perseverance and supplication for all the
saints" (Eph. 6:18).

What is that we are to pray? We are to call on the name of
the Lord and pray for His deliverance. We are to ask Him to
defeat the devil in our lives and to act in victorious strength
and power on our behalf.

You may be asking, "Can a child engage in spiritual warfare?" Yes! A child can be taught from the earliest ages to put
on the whole armor of God and to resist the devil. We are wise
to teach our children how to put on the armor of God in a way
that is literal to them—imagining that they are putting on a
helmet, a breastplate, and so forth as they recite and memorize Ephesians 6:14–17. In this way, they not only feel stronger
in their faith and more courageous as they face the world each
day, but they have a visual image to help them remember all
their lives that their strength lies totally in Christ Jesus. Furthermore, your child *can* resist the devil and *can* pray! Even a
young child can be taught to pray, "Help me, God!"

Encourage your child that as he resists the devil, the devil
must flee from him (see James 4:7). Encourage your child also
that Jesus is the Deliverer from all evil, all the time.

What the Word Says

Resist the devil and he will flee

What the Word Says to Me

----

from you. Draw near to God
and He will draw near to you.
(James 4:7–8)

[Jesus said,] "The thief does
not come except to steal, and
to kill, and to destroy. I have
come that they may have life,
and that they may have it more
abundantly." (John 10:10)

And it shall come to pass
That whoever calls on the
name of the LORD
Shall be saved. (Joel 2:32)

A child who learns how to overcome both unpleasant situations and genuine problems lives confidently, boldly, and with inner strength, courage, peace, and joy. Such a child may be temporarily fearful but need never give in to fear. What a wonderful legacy to leave your children!

- *What insights do you have into the legacy God desires for you to leave your children?*

- *In what ways are you feeling challenged in your spirit?*

TEN

GETTING INTO POSITION TO RECEIVE GOD'S REWARDS

Every parent I know desires for his or her child to be "successful" in life. But what does that means in terms of leaving a legacy to a child? From the Bible standpoint, it means training your child to be a good steward of all his resources—first and foremost, his *life*—and to be a generous giver to God's work and to those in need. Good stewardship and generosity are the keys that unlock God's storehouse of blessing!

Good Stewardship

As a foundation for good stewardship, we are wise to teach our children to have a right attitude about money, the use of material possessions, and the relationship between faith and work.

1. *Our attitude toward money must be free of envy, greed, and idolatry.* Many people make "things" into idols. They live to

acquire things; they base their self-esteem upon the possession of material goods—from wearing the "right" labels to driving the "right" kind of car; they routinely compare their possessions to the possessions of others; and they habitually are unhappy with what they have and desire more.

Teach your child that God comes first . . . always! Jesus taught,

> "But seek first the kingdom of God and His righteousness, and all these things shall be added to you." (Matt. 6:33)

Our emphasis in life is to be on the pursuit of those things that are eternal, not on things that rust, wear out, or rot away (see Matt. 6:20–21).

What the Word Says	What the Word Says to Me
I am the LORD your God . . . You shall have no other gods before Me. (Exod. 20:2–3)	------------------------------- ------------------------------- -------------------------------
Flee from idolatry. (1 Cor. 10:14)	------------------------------- -------------------------------
You shall not covet your neighbor's house; you shall not covet your neighbor's wife, nor his manservant, nor his maidservant, nor his ox, nor his donkey, nor anything that is your neighbor's. (Exod. 20:17)	------------------------------- ------------------------------- ------------------------------- ------------------------------- ------------------------------- ------------------------------- -------------------------------
Let your conduct be without covetousness, and be content with such things as you have. (Heb. 13:5)	------------------------------- ------------------------------- ------------------------------- -------------------------------

He who is greedy for gain
troubles his own house. (Prov.
15:27)

[Jesus said,] "Do not lay up for
yourselves treasures on earth,
where moth and rust destroy
and where thieves break in and
steal; but lay up for yourselves
treasures in heaven, where neither moth nor rust destroys
and where thieves do not break
in and steal. For where your
treasures is, there your heart
will be also." (Matt. 6:19–21)

2. *Our position toward money should be neutral—it is what we* do *with money that counts.* Money and material possessions in and of themselves are neither good nor bad. God is far more concerned about the attitudes and desires we have toward money than He is about our current bank statements. Are we trusting in our riches for security? Are we hoarding possessions in fear of being without sufficient supply? Are we holding back from doing good with our money in selfishness? Are we so consumed with the idea of making money and buying things that we ignore our relationship with God? These are attitudes that God desires us to overcome!

To a great extent, a child adopts the attitude of his parents toward money and material possessions. Reflect upon your own attitude toward money and material goods. Your attitude is the attitude your child will mimic.

What the Word Says

What the Word Says to Me

As he thinks in his heart, so is
he. (Prov. 23:7)

Therefore, as we have opportunity, let us do good to all, especially to those who are of the household of faith. (Gal. 6:10)

Their feet run to evil,
And they make haste to shed blood.
Surely, in vain the net is spread
In the sight of any bird;
But they lie in wait for their own blood,
They lurk secretly for their own lives.
So are the ways of everyone who is greedy for gain;
It takes away the life of its owners. (Prov. 1:16–19)

3. *We are commanded to work honestly.* The Bible clearly states that able-bodied and capable people are to work and provide for their own needs. It speaks very strongly against procrastination, laziness, slothfulness, and an unwillingness to be diligent in work. As a parent, we are wise to teach our children how to work and to value work. Children should be given various responsibilities and chores around the house and, at appropriate times, should be encouraged to earn part of their spending money. Reward your child for jobs well done with praise and words of appreciation. Require your child to work honestly and with integrity.

What the Word Says

What the Word Says to Me

Wealth gained by dishonesty will be diminished,

But he who gathers by labor
will increase. (Prov. 13:11)

We urge you, brethren, that
you increase more and more;
that you also aspire to lead a
quiet life, to mind your own
business, and to work with
your own hands, as we commanded you, that you may
walk properly toward those
who are outside, and that you
may lack nothing. (1 Thess.
4:10–12)

If anyone will not work, neither shall he eat. For we hear
that there are some who walk
among you in a disorderly
manner, not working at all, but
are busybodies. Now those
who are such we command
and exhort through our Lord
Jesus Christ that they work in
quietness and eat their own
bread. (2 Thess. 3:10–12)

Whatever your hand finds to
do, do it with your might.
(Eccles. 9:10)

The hand of the diligent will
rule,
But the slothful will be put to
forced labor. (Prov. 12:24)

4. *We are commanded to trust God to provide what we need and to guide our work.* Teach your child to give his best effort to honest work, and then to trust God to provide ample reward for his work. Help your child discover the work that is best suited to his natural God-given talents and abilities, and to become trained and skilled in that area of work. Pray with your child that God will give your child wisdom, strength, and enthusiasm for work and that your child will be able to maintain a high level of quality in all he undertakes.

What the Word Says

You shall rejoice in all to which you have put your hand, you and your households, in which the LORD your God has blessed you. (Deut. 12:7)

Let us not grow weary while doing good, for in due season we shall reap if we do not lose heart. (Gal. 6:9)

What the Word Says to Me

_____

_____

_____

_____

_____

_____

_____

_____

_____

• *Identify your emotional responses to these words:*

Work

_____

_____

Prosperity

_____

_____

Greed

_____

_____

Generosity in Giving

Make "giving" a part of your child's training from his earliest days. Teach your child to be obedient in giving to God's work, and encourage your child to be *generous* toward others who are in need. The Bible teaches, "God loves a cheerful giver" (2 Cor. 9:7).

Those who give generously are those who receive generously. This does not mean that a person should give themselves into indebtedness. Nor should our giving ever be done to gain the approval of others. Our giving is to be like our work and our obedience: *as to the Lord.*

Make sure your child has something to put into the offering plate each Sunday when he goes to church. If your child is receiving an allowance or payment for work, encourage your child to give a tithe (one-tenth) to the Lord. One of the clearest passages in the Bible about giving is in Malachi 3:8–12, and what a promise is included in that passage for those who tithe faithfully!

"Will a man rob God?
Yet you have robbed Me!
But you say,
'In what way have we robbed You?'
In tithes and offerings.
You are cursed with a curse,
For you have robbed Me,
Even this whole nation.
Bring all the tithes into the storehouse,
That there may be food in My house,
And prove Me now in this,"
Says the LORD of hosts,
"If I will not open for you the windows of heaven
And pour out for you such blessing
That there will not be room enough to receive it.

And I will rebuke the devourer for your sakes,
So that he will not destroy the fruit of your ground,

Nor shall the vine fail to bear fruit for you in the field,"
Says the LORD of hosts;
"And all nations will call you blessed,
For you will be a delightful land,"
Says the LORD of hosts.

God expects every person to tithe—the tithe is given to God *from* our increase and *for* our increase. It is the way we open the door of our finances to give and then to receive God's blessing and to renew God's blessing into our lives. It is an act of our faith that we are trusting God to grow the "seed" we plant and to cause it to multiply on our behalf.

The child who learns to give generously to the Lord's work and to others he sees in need is a child who becomes unselfish. Such a child is going to receive great blessings, not only from God, but from other people.

* *What new insights do you have into this passage from Malachi?*

_____

_____

What the Word Says	What the Word Says to Me
Do not be deceived, God is not mocked; for whatever a man sows, that he will also reap. (Gal. 6:7)	_____ _____ _____ _____
He who sows sparingly will also reap sparingly, and he who sows bountifully will also reap bountifully. (2 Cor. 9:6)	_____ _____ _____ _____
[Jesus said,] "Freely you have received, freely give." (Matt. 10:8)	_____ _____ _____

[Jesus said,] "Give, and it will be given to you: good measure, pressed down, shaken together, and running over will be put into your bosom. For with the same measure that you use, it will be measured back to you." (Luke 6:38)

Honor the LORD with your possessions,
And with the firstfruits of all your increase;
So your barns will be filled with plenty,
And your vats will overflow with new wine. (Prov. 3:9–10)

So let each one give as he purposes in his heart, not grudgingly or of necessity; for God loves a cheerful giver. And God is able to make all grace abound toward you, that you, always having all sufficiency in all things, have an abundance for every good work. (2 Cor. 9:7–8)

Jesus taught very specific things about our giving. These are key principles to teach your children:

- We are to give to the needy, wherever we find them (Matt. 25:37–40).
- We are to give sacrificially (Mark 12:41–44).

- We are to give without a great public display or show (Matt. 6:1–4).
- It is more blessed to give than to receive (Acts 20:35).

While the tithe is the standard for giving to God's work, we must always recognize the truth of 1 Chronicles 29:14: "All things come from You, and of Your own we have given You." Everything we have and are is a gift of God to us, and *all* of what we are and have belongs to God for His use at *all* times.

A child who is trained to be a generous giver and a good steward of all that he has been given from God—his time, his talents, his resources, his energy, his love—is a child who is going to live not only in sufficiency but in *satisfaction and fulfillment.* What a wonderful legacy it is for a child to be taught *how* to give and receive from God!

- *What new insights do you have into the legacy you are to leave your children?*

_____

_____

- *In what ways are you feeling challenged in your spirit?*

_____

_____

YOUR CHILDREN FOLLOW IN YOUR FOOTSTEPS

As we have noted repeatedly in this study, your children follow in *your* footsteps. As influential as a pastor, teacher, or other adult may be in a child's life, nobody can leave a legacy to a child in the same way you can as a parent.

Ask the Lord to help you today to leave to your child the legacy *He* desires for you to leave. No parent is a perfect parent—such a person has never existed and never will exist. Every parent has faults and failures. What we must do as parents is to trust God to help us, to guide us, and to do for our child what we as parents are incapable of doing. We are to trust God to work all things together for the good of our child (Rom. 8:28).

Desire today to be the best parent you can possibly be and to leave the greatest spiritual legacy you can possibly leave to your child. And then give your efforts to the Lord and trust Him to use your example and your teaching in whatever ways He desires to bring about the perfection and completion of your child. God's ultimate goal is to see your child grow to maturity in the likeness of Jesus Christ. Make that your goal, too!